Kibbutz Journal

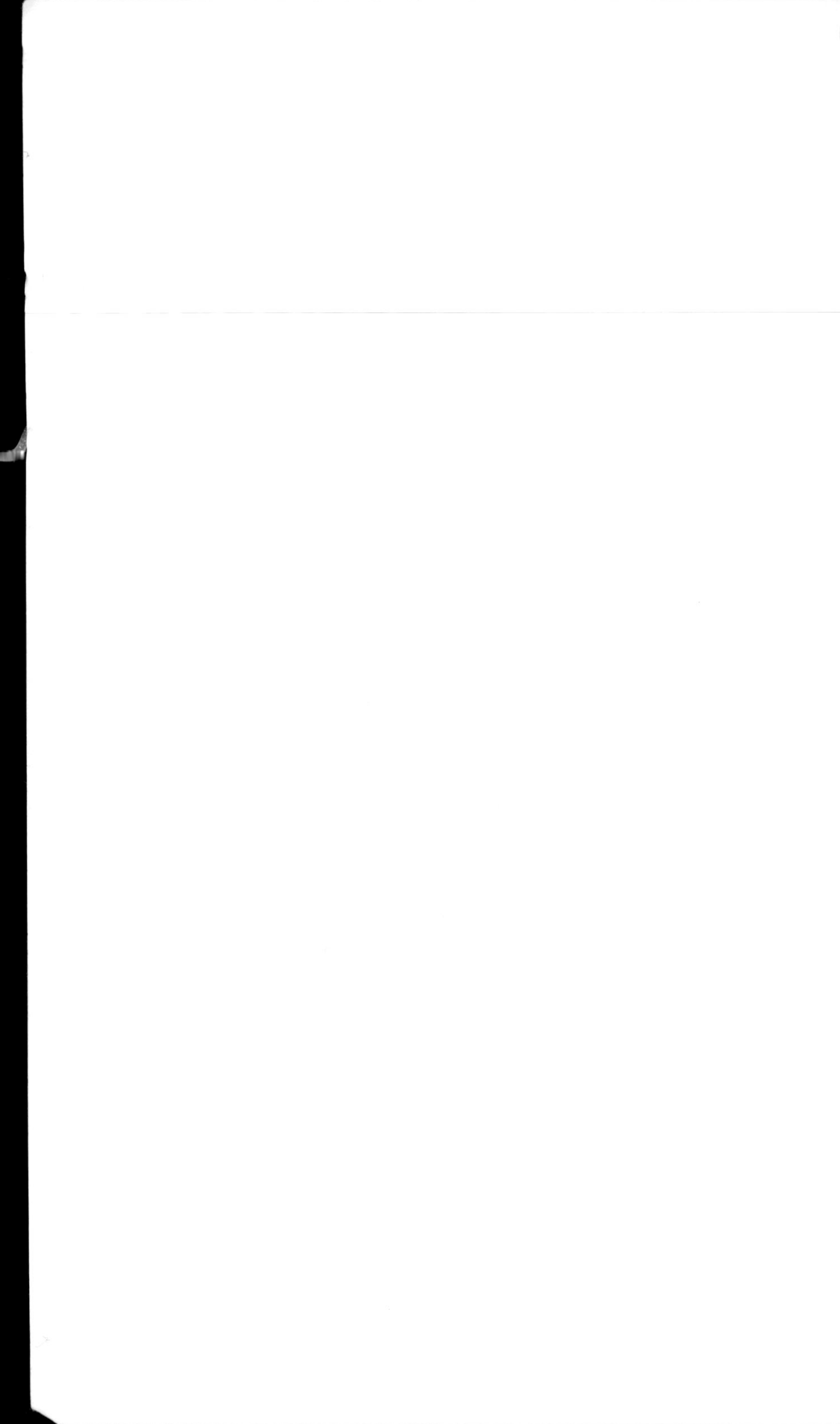

KIBBUTZ JOURNAL

Reflections on Gender, Race & Militarism in Israel

Kathy E. Ferguson

TRILOGY
BOOKS

Pasadena, California

 For information, address Trilogy Books, 50 S. DeLacey Avenue, Suite 201, Pasadena, CA 91105.

Cover Photo credits: "Fighters at the Western Wall" courtesy of Palphot, Ltd.; "Women in Black" courtesy of Breirot.

Cover design: J. Stevens Art & Design

Publisher's Cataloging in Publication

Ferguson, Kathy E.

Kibbutz journal: reflections on gender, race & militarism in Israel / Kathy E. Ferguson.

p. cm.

Includes bibliographical references

ISBN 0-9623879-6-7

1. Israel--History. 2. Man-woman relationships--Israel. 3. Jewish-Arab relations. 4. Militarism--Israel. I. Title.

DS126.5.F47 1995 956.94'05'4

QBI94-21221

Library of Congress Catalog Card Number: 94-61802

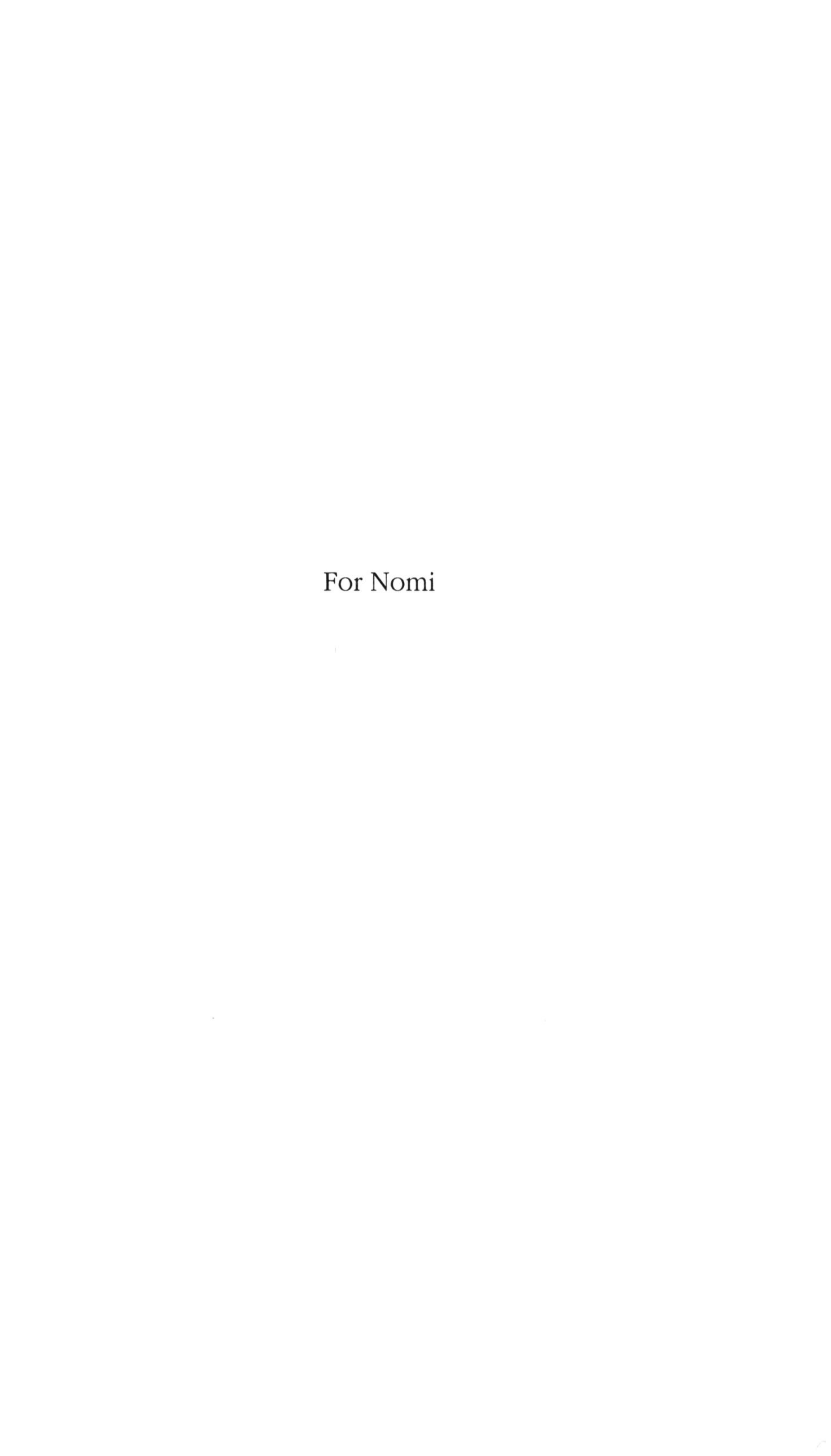

For Nomi

Author's Note

This journal was written during a four-month stay on a kibbutz in central/southern Israel. I have changed the names of friends and family members on the kibbutz, and disguised the identity of the kibbutz itself, to protect the privacy of those involved. I have not changed the names of individuals who are already public figures—intellectuals, activists, and political leaders.

Acknowledgements

My deepest thanks to my old friend Cindy Carson for her careful, critical readings of this journal and for her companionship in the adventure of writing. Jane Bennett, Joan Catapano, Carol Cohn, Carolyn DiPalma, Cynthia Enloe, Margaret Osburn, Chris Robinson, Joan Robinson, Mike Shapiro, Gila Svirsky and Phyllis Turnbull were all generous in the time they gave to the manuscript and thoughtful in their comments. I appreciate the critical and supportive remarks of the students in my feminist theory classes, especially Pam Hiyashi. Thanks also to Gina Buschmann, Peggy Cox, Leon Halpert, Hilary Lamishaw, and Dawn Suyenaga for taking the time to read it. Thanks very much to Kennan Ferguson for turning me on to Art Spiegelman's *Maus* series.

I am grateful to the feminists I have met in Israel who shared both their political passions and their intellectual insights with me. Galia Golan, Naomi Graetz, Sarit Helman, Elena Loory, Tamar Rapoport, Erella Shadmi, Anita Steiner, Gila Svirsky, and Niza Yanay not only assisted with this project but also helped me begin to make an intellectual home for myself in Israel.

Gili, Oren, and Ari have, in their different ways, helped me to map the terrain we encountered together in Israel. Gili provided the occasion for my first connections with Israel, while Oren and Ari have both tightened and troubled the bond.

I owe my greatest debt of thanks to our family and friends on our kibbutz. They have made me welcome and shared their lives with me. While they will not agree with much that I have written here, I hope they will take this journal as a small gesture of return.

Introduction
Borders, Voices, and the Traffic In Between

LIFE IN ISRAEL brings one into intimate contact with a variety of borders and an intense set of claims about identity. There are the obvious physical borders, the ones between disputed territories and hostile states, where people cross between contested places in search of work, or in the line of duty, or for renewal or revenge. Then there are the seemingly obvious cultural borders between contending identities, between Arab and Jew, women and men, immigrant and native-born, religious and secular, dove and hawk. These too turn out to be contested spaces, hosting their own, often clandestine, border crossings. And then there are the furtive borders, woven into language practices and written onto bodies, which demarcate that which can be spoken from that which lies in silence.

This journal is an effort to engage these borders, to map their inclusions and exclusions, to chart the migrations they sustain and to attend to the utterances they authorize or forbid. These efforts are both informed and complicated, perhaps sometimes derailed, by the borders of my own inhabitations—a U.S. academic living on a kibbutz, a *goya* (non-Jew) marrying into an Israeli Jewish family, a feminist in the place that may well have invented patriarchy. These deceptively straightforward traits seem to confirm my outsider status. But I cannot stay comfortably outside Israeli Jewish life, because my children have one set of roots, one cherished link with family, one opening to language and memory, in this troubled and troubling place. This journal has become my forum for negotiating a peaceful identity space for my sons, a kind of belonging that is living and livable for them and for myself. Constructing these terms for Oren and Ari requires mapping the available practices by which identity is constructed in Israeli life. I find these practices to be complex, appealing, disturbing, in some ways unacceptable. I want to close the distance between us and Israel, but not always on Israel's terms.

The most consistent anchor I have found in these negotiations is that of a mother of sons who in some ways belong in Israel. While of course other identity positions come into play, mothering recurs as my most compelling point of departure because it is as a mother that these questions most desperately matter to me. Mapping the identity practices of others can be an arrogant and judgmental act, the casual critical glance of the cross-cultural tourist. The concrete concerns of mothering require a more nuanced involvement: I cannot either dismiss or embrace the cultural terrain this journal charts.

But the terrain of mothering is itself fraught with difficulties. It is thoroughly overcoded with sentimentality, usually thought to be the opposite of rational deliberation. It seems to invite a biological misinterpretation in which appeals to a physical essence (e.g., "maternal instinct") replace analyses of a cultural practice. It marks a kind of power that is as capable of abuse as any other. It is deeply sunk into a cultural nexus that readily becomes maudlin about mothers while denying any real power to women. Mothering itself requires continuous reinterpretation in order to be inhabitable. While mothering guarantees no foundation, it provides both a potent starting point and a besieged investment. Mothering, critically construed, offers both my strongest motives and my most ambivalent tools in this effort to plot the topographies of identity available in Israel.

But of course there is no one Israel. There is more than one discernible voice, more than one detectable construction of who lives here and what they are about. A state or a society is never a simple or static thing; it is always a process of becoming. Global politics tends to be understood in unitary terms—i.e., we say "Israel" acts in a certain way on the world stage—but that common, one-dimensional way of speaking conceals great turbulence. One of the tasks of the Israeli state has been to mask this turbulence by defending its borders—geographic, cultural, linguistic—in ways that co-opt or delegitimize its subversions. The less common views are hard to hear when the hegemonic voices are turned up to full volume. The dominant view becomes deafening, but the less legitimized views continue to intersect the identity practices in complex ways. They do their work on the slant, so to speak, uncaptured by the prevailing orthodoxy, but not unaffected by it.

On one level, the landscape of Israeli political and cultural life is amazingly diverse. There are the differences among/between the many languages of the immigrants and the official Hebrew; between *sabra* (Israeli-born) Hebrew and the Yiddish of the *shtetl*; between Hebrew and the widespread use of English in commerce, tourism, and Diaspora fundraising; between Hebrew and the subterranean Arabic of the nearly one million Israeli Arabs (not counting the population of the occupied territories). There are also the discrepancies and antagonisms within the Hebrew-speaking population: between Ashkenazi (European) and Sephardic (Mediterranean) Jews, secular and religious Jews, conservative and radical Jews, Jewish women and Jewish men. There are the subtle contests between the available linguistic registers within which self-understanding can be constituted: between the images of globalism and nationalism, victims and warriors, remembrance and forgetting, nostalgia and irony. The self-understandings that people can articulate within Israeli society always hum with the energies of these interacting interpretive moments; the words they can speak are always already half someone else's.

Set against this unruly cacophony are the agents of unification—the state, the rabbinate, the media, the schools—and the relentless unifying drone of the discourse of "national security." On this level, the centralizing forces work at corralling the diversity within Israeli life, and thus at reinforcing the reigning claims to meaning. Further harnessing the dominant self-understanding is a particularly strident masculinity, a gendered underwriting of the central order. The dominant cultural forces are threatened by the manyness of things, the differences which put constant pressure on prevailing truth claims and self-understandings. The agents of unification attempt to tame the fractious dialogues, to marshal the (selective) resources of history, geography and culture around a single understanding of what it means to be Israeli.

Mapping the spaces upon which these forces interrupt and reinforce one another requires detecting the resonances and incompatibilities among various ways of representing the world, and between ways of representing the world and ways of being in the world. One looks for the symbolic markers by which people establish and assess their sense of themselves. This way of looking at global politics seeks the locations in language that constitute people's sense of pride or shame, their fears and expectations, their resistances and resignations. It looks at the practices of power involved in struggles to maintain, and to reformulate, identities.

Mapping identity practices is a dangerous business in that the people whose self-representations one is scrutinizing are always more than those representations. Identity practices are not the same as personalities. Rather, they are the cultural network of symbols and codes within which their residents must navigate. There is always slippage and contestation among the recurrent images anchoring the available understandings people have of themselves and others. One can locate such slippage by following identities as they travel, contrasting their reception in different contexts in order more fully to chart their relations. Encounters among different languages offer a space for reflection on the requirements of each. Identities on the move highlight the construction of the cultural categories they encounter, and might even occasion their reconstruction.

April 6, 1992

Today I begin my journal of this stay on the kibbutz. We've been here about two weeks, in a whirl of settling in, getting the kids started in the kindergarten and the children's house, enrolling me in an *ulpan* (Hebrew school for immigrants), arranging Gili's work at the mechanic's shop. Oren will go to the *gan* (kindergarten) with the other five- and six-year-olds; he's already begun to make friends with Sidra, my friend Vickie's oldest daughter. Ari will be at the infant's house with the other babies. We have a spacious house of our own, pleasantly furnished by Gili's parents and sisters, on the edge of the kibbutz near the cattle pastures. There is a rope swing in front of our house, where the children from this block of houses gather to play. Each house has a bit of garden attached; most are carefully attended, while ours is among the more anarchic. We dug into the hard soil and planted marigolds to go with the many other flowers cultivated by the previous residents.

The kibbutz is a blaze of color, thanks to the very wet winter. There are flowers everywhere, lush and fragrant. The kibbutz is verdant, full of life. This festival of color requires a double vision—to appreciate its fertile beauty, in this place of near desert; and to recall the (nearly) invisible costs—Arab homes abandoned in their flight from what they saw as Israeli occupation some 40 years ago; Palestinian camps in Gaza that lack the water flowing so abundantly over kibbutz gardens.

All of Israel requires this double, triple, multiple vision—which Israel? Whose? Where and when? Some months ago I got a very moving letter from my old pal

Leon about his family's trip from New York to Israel. His father, a survivor of the camps, found a kind of home and peace in this land, perhaps some respite from the haunting past. Meanwhile, the strong young men of the kibbutz go off to serve their time in the reserves; they come and go, matter-of-factly integrating their military service into their daily lives, serving their time with little comment. Often they become taciturn when asked about their experiences in the reserves. Do they take part in the torture of Palestinians detained in the occupied territories? Do they only turn a deaf ear to the tortures that others inflict? Do they have more sanitary work, something more removed from the daily labor of controlling and intimidating a population? When asked, Omer, Gili's old classmate, smiles his ready, charming smile and indicates that he only drives a jeep in training maneuvers. What past will haunt him?

A recent edition of the *Jerusalem Post* carries three articles on its back page: the first two describe "terrorist" attacks by Palestinians against Jews, either military or civilian; the third details a charge by *B'Tselem*, an Israeli/Jewish human rights organization, of continuing torture of Palestinians arrested by the authorities, including sleep deprivation and "severe beatings." The production of "terrorist" and "state" is enacted on these pages. A Palestinian is arrested for attacking a Jewish farmer, and is quoted as saying he wants to "kill Jews." No Jews have to say they want to kill Arabs—the state does it for them, in the name of civil order. The Palestinians have no legitimate order of their own, on whose behalf they can act; they are the terrorists. No claims of self defense, such as those the Israeli military makes for its soldiers, are recognized for them.

I began my *ulpan* yesterday. I share a class with two Brits, one other woman from the U.S., one Chilean, one Argentinean, and six "Russians" (they are all referred to as Russians by Israelis, although they come from many different areas of the former Soviet Union). We are learning some elementary claims about identity, such as: "Now I am a student in an *ulpan* in Israel. In America I am a teacher." This is unproblematic for me, since I will go back to "America" and be a teacher again. I wonder what the immigrants think, what dislocations of identity are named in these simple exercises. They will not ever go back to Russia and be an electrical engineer, a conductor, a baker; they may never do those things again. Israel has little opportunity for its immigrant professionals. What jagged tears are unsutured in these simple sentences: Now I am a student in Israel; in Russia I am a conductor of music.

April 12

I'VE BEEN WORKING on the letter I'm sending out to people about my research. Political questions keep coming up in the wording of the letters. I am saying that I want to work on feminism and anti-militarism "here." I wonder, where will these people think that I think "here" is? Israel? Palestine? A disputed place? I finally said "Israel and the occupied territories" to indicate that "here" is not just one place, not a settled place. Then I wondered, does it matter if I capitalize occupied territories? After all, I capitalize Israel. What is the convention among citizens? Activists? Whose agenda am I supporting, and whose am I contesting, with these gestures? Will I ever completely know, and do I even want to?

This is exhausting. My letters say that I want to interview "women, Israeli and Palestinian, who are active..." Then I thought, why not just say "Israeli and Palestinian women"? Putting the adjectives in a qualifying clause somehow marks them off, as though I were congratulating myself for including both groups. Or is it only my political paranoia that would suspect such motives? Dancing through the minefield. . . .

I read an editorial in the *Jerusalem Post* about how great the "Christian Zionists" in the U.S. are because they give strong support to Israel. The editors should go to the part of Indiana where I grew up and meet some of these Christian Zionists—people who love Israel for narrow ideological reasons (Israel has to exist before the second coming can happen) but they don't much care for Jews. These Christian Zionists will support the likes of the Likud and Shamir with all kinds of money and political pressure, without a thought about what that does for prospects of peace here, and certainly with no concern for the Palestinians. After all, the Bible doesn't order up a homeland for them as prerequisite for a second coming.

It looks like its going to be a choice between Bush and Clinton for President in the U.S. I can't possibly vote for Bush, not after the Gulf War, the CIA stuff, Nicaragua, etc., etc., *ad nauseum.* But Bush seems better on Israel than Clinton—at least Bush is willing to put some pressure on Shamir and the Israeli right to talk to the Palestinians. Aviv, my brother-in-law, asked me why. I'm not sure, but I think maybe because the oil supply seems secure, the U.S. feels superior after invading Iraq, and Arab unity seems pretty fragile and unthreatening to U.S. hegemony, so peace talks don't look so dangerous. My friend Chris insists its a deal Bush made with the Arab nations for their backing against Iraq. Maybe Bush is getting tired of spending the millions of dollars it takes DAILY to prop up Israel. Clinton, on the other hand, seems to have totally bought the U.S. Israeli lobby's line that unquestioning support for Israel's right wing government is the only way to "support Israel." At least, that is how the early campaign talk sounds over here, filtered through the lens of the *Jerusalem Post.*

April 14

Recently we were treated to a very lively lecture on Israel's government at the *ulpan.* A large, florid, friendly man from a local kibbutz talked about the complex workings of the parliamentary system. I have always admired proportional representation because it allows for more diversity to be voiced within the political system, and gives the smaller parties a chance to be heard. The Green Party, for instance, would do a lot better in the U.S. if we did not have our winner-take-all system of Congressional elections. The flip side of this, of course, is that it also allows the small parties from the other end of the political spectrum to wield considerable weight. In Israel the ultra-nationalist, ultra-religious parties on the far right have extraordinary clout because their withdrawal of support can cripple the governing coalition.

Our speaker explained the complex evolution of Israel's multiparty coalition system with a charming combination of national pride and self-deprecating humor, reminding me of Gili's old joke that when you put two Israelis into a room you get three political parties. He reminded us frequently that Israel is "the only democracy in the Middle East." In many ways this claim is true; but it requires a number of silences to sustain it. Our speaker failed to address either the second class citizenship of the Israeli Arabs, or the intimate power of the Orthodox religious authorities over much of daily life. Perhaps it is an American conceit that democracy requires separation of church and state; but women and non-Jews are clearly disadvantaged by the strong influence of the rabbinate over education and family life. Nor was there any mention of the effect of conducting a military occupation on democratic processes at home.

April 19

IT'S EASTER TODAY. I'm making an Easter Egg Hunt for Oren and his cousins, much to the puzzlement of the rest of the family. Today I went to the market in Sderot with Narkis, Gili's older sister, and we saw a balloon shaped like a rabbit. I suggested that it was the Easter Bunny, and Narkis hadn't a clue what I was talking about. It's a bit hard to explain the Easter bunny, even without our language inadequacies.

Pessah is a cheerful, lively holiday. The kibbutz has a long celebration Friday night, with lots of people reading and singing songs. The young children look for the *afikoman* (hidden matzoh bread) and march through the dining room waving bundles of straw. There is a very nice spirit on this kibbutz, very friendly, warm and happy. Dov (Gili's father) and a buddy of his sang a noisy, lively song, with help from Ari, who "sang" along on his own. And the food was great.

Yesterday we went with Dov, Simon (Dov's brother, visiting from South America) and Lana (his wife) to Yad Mordechai, a nearby kibbutz where the kibbutzniks held off the invading Egyptian army in 1948 for several days. Their actions gave the towns farther north, including Tel Aviv, time to prepare for the invasion. There is a field containing statues of Egyptian soldiers charging up the hills, with their tanks and heavy artillery. The trenches at the top of the hill hold reproductions of the scant kibbutz armaments. There's also a museum to the memory of the Holocaust and the Yad Mordechai fighters. The claims on memory are heavy: defending the new state from the invading Arab armies is all intertwined with the Holocaust and the struggle in the Polish ghettos against the Nazis. In each case the story features the underdog Jewish fighters who have some temporary successes against a larger and very evil enemy, and in each case their immediate defeat paves the way for a long-term victory. The setting for memory at Yad Mordechai contributes to maintenance of the Israeli understanding of themselves as beleaguered underdogs, victims constantly threatened. It allows them to dislocate this identity from its moorings in 1942 or 1948 and float it into place in 1992, so that the Palestinians (and their supporters, and anyone who ever criticizes Israel) become the feared enemy and the Jews are still the victims.

An oppressive state gives its dominant classes many alibis for their superior position. State censorship and economic segregation makes the Palestinians invisible to most Israeli Jews. For some, the Bible (and not the Koran) is taken to be a land-granting institution. Evocations of biblical legends shore up contemporary claims to land and power. What to do with a people who remember events from 3000 years ago as though they happened last week? A recent *Jerusalem Post* article sees Hebron as a likely place for Jews and Arabs to make peace because Abraham's sons Isaac (Jewish) and Ismael (Arab) both buried him near there. (I think I've gotten that story right.) Anyway, that seems a bit removed from the contemporary situation to me; but then I'm a U.S. American, inflicted with the opposite problem, no historical memory at all. I think Nietzsche may have been right about the virtues of forgetting, at least sometimes. Israelis and Palestinians seem to go, instead, with Hegel—remember everything. My understanding of

Hebron is that it is an Arab city in the occupied territories and is a less than promising site for mutual understanding.

At Yad Mordechai, there is a photo of a list of deportees to Auschwitz. Dov's and Simon's mother's surname and grandmother's surname appear on that list. Oren and Ari probably have relatives who died at Auschwitz. Someday they must know this. My sons live in a world in which, not so long ago, to be the son of a Jew was a death sentence. It could happen again. If they come to live in Israel, they will be asked, in the name of that memory, to kill and oppress the sons and daughters of Palestinians. It is happening now. Living as they do in Hawaii, in a predominantly non-Jewish setting, Oren and Ari will have to be taught to remember; if they lived in Israel, it would be the practices of forgetting that they would need to cultivate. And if we move back to Indiana, with my family, a different sort of local knowledge would demand remembering; Indiana has an enthusiastic past and present relationship with the Ku Klux Klan, and the surnames of relatives might well appear on those lists too.

We went to the border of Gaza yesterday. We did not go in. Photos were forbidden. It was desolate, a stark military check point on a dusty land. Sometimes the serenity of the kibbutz chokes me. Dov often drives the Palestinians who work in the kibbutz factory ("our Arabs") home; he locks his doors and hurries, driven by fear. Unease for one's own safety blocks sight of institutionalized violence.

April 20

OREN AND I went with Simon, Lana and Dov to the magnificent Soreq caves in the Absolom Reserve. Awesome stalagmites and stalactites haunt the caves, and the air is wet and full of mystery. At the concession stand I found, much to Oren's delight, M&Ms for sale; I also found some fascinating productions of Israeli identity on the tourist postcards.

In among the wide angle landscape shots of the Sea of Galilee and Masada were two cards also evidently deemed by the Israeli tourist industry to be fitting mementos for visitors and the folks back home. One shows a close-up of a sabra, a cactus with large flat leaves and round, orange fruit. The caption states "The renowned Israeli sabra cactus, symbol of the Israeli temperament: prickly on the outside, sweet on the inside." Behind the cactus stand two young, attractive women in military uniform; wearing red flowers on their shirts, they stride forward with confidence and exchange friendly smiles. The cloudless blue sky shines brightly behind them. The card radiates reassurance. The military trappings on the cheerful young women are quintessentially Israeli, the prickly "outside" hiding the sweet feminine "inside." The women, like the cactus, are "in bloom," sporting flowers, promising new life. The young women smile at each other, happy with life; their military presence is folded into that contentment; all is well with the Israeli army, where beautiful young women serve their country with a smile. There is no mention of women's second class status in the military, their obligatory presence there in perpetual subordination to men. No sign of what these charming, attractive soldiers might actually be doing, which is probably to staff the clerical ranks of the Israeli war machine. Do they, perhaps, call up the reserve soldiers who police Gaza? Do they keep the files on suspected "terrorists"? Do they consider their hands to be clean? They wear their jaunty red caps at a dashing angle; they are proud and strong. Their beauty and boldness resides robustly in their military uniforms; the military presence is unremarkable in itself, imbricated thoroughly into what it means to be an Israeli.

A second postcard reproduces a reassuring militarized identity from a different angle. It shows three men, each wearing green military fatigues and sporting a different colored beret—purple, red, brown. They stand with arms clasped around one another, backs to the camera, their faces hidden against a wall. Not "a wall"—"THE Wall." The caption reads "Meeting of fighters at the Western Wall." Their faces are pressed up against the white-gold Jerusalem stone, which gleams hot in the sun. Their weapons hang from their shoulders; they appear to be weeping. Their bodies are slim and strong, their arms well-muscled; they are strong enough to cry, perhaps for a fallen comrade, perhaps even for a slain enemy. Again, Israeli strength and youth, this time marked masculine, is interwoven with fatigues and weapons; to be a real Israeli IS to be a soldier. In Israeli postcard iconography, the women soldiers are strong enough to serve their country, to BE Israeli, with a smile; the men soldiers are strong enough to grieve at the costs of their military service while continuing to provide it. Serve, serve, serve; little room here to recognize young people with a different dream, a different strength. Little room for some other kind of Israeli.

The second postcard represents a line of Israeli kitsch going back at least to the creation of Zionism. In "The Kitsch of Israel" Avishai Margalit tells about a "bizarre controversy" in 1988 over the question "Should soldiers be allowed to cry at the funerals of their comrades?"

> The general who opposed crying—or, more exactly, being seen crying—was a sabra born on a kibbutz; the one in favor of showing soldiers crying was a Polish-born survivor of the Holocaust. . . . The argument about the soldiers' tears goes to the heart of

> a fundamental issue about sentimentality in the Zionist revolution, the revolution that took it upon itself to mold a "New Jew." The New Jew was not supposed to shed tears. (p. 20)

For the sabra general, tears recall the helpless Jews of the ghettos and pogroms, history's victims. His rejection of public vulnerability aligns Jewish victimization with a no-nonsense, "stop whining and do something about it" revision. The Polish-born general is more representative of immigrant and Diaspora Jews, the archetype of a righteous sentimentality. Sometimes this emotional register takes a universal turn, as in the *mensch*-ideal, a good guy who is sensitive to the suffering of others. But more often it is channeled by state-orchestrated ideological production lines into an insular tribalism, as in the "we-love-Israel, the-world-is-against-us" form of self-justification. (p. 21)

No one in this debate suggests that the military does not need a policy about soldiers crying or not crying, that such matters are private and none of the state's business. The production and deployment of images of young people in uniform is so central to Israeli self-understanding, and so critical to its marketing of itself abroad, not to mention to its ideological and commercial tourism, that the constitution of the phenomenon as a public issue was self-evident. The postcard Oren and I secured along with our M&Ms is the heir of countless photographs, poems, songs, books, legends. Margalit writes:

> The quasi-official symbol [of soldiers and sentiment] became the photograph by the veteran *Time* photographer David Rubinger which shows a group of unshaven helmeted paratroopers at the wall, in the middle of which one sees—*ecce homo*—a young, blond, lean-featured fighter with his eyes

> lifted upward and holding his helmet next to his heart. This altogether non-Jewish gesture of taking off one's hat at a holy place became the symbol of the return of the New Jew to the site of his holy temple. (p. 20)

Margalit also indicates some of the sources of resistance to the earnest images of self-satisfaction. A popular rock song by female performer Sy Hyman criticizes the saccharine, sanctimonious tone of the "Shooting and Crying" literature, as does poet Dennis Silk in "On the Way to the Territories." Hyman's song is banned from the army radio station in Israel.(pp. 20, 22) I remember some of Gili's stories about his days in the military, his indifference to patriotic exhortations and his small gestures of defiance. Yoram Binur's descriptions of his lackadaisical performance in the military in *My Enemy, My Self* are a refreshing change from most such memoirs, which seem to combine gung-ho soldiering with just the right touch of moral reflection. It is crucial to keep evidence of these resistances and interruptions in mind, both to help explain the continuous onslaught of the prevailing identity practices and to marshal some resources against them.

In Israeli military kitsch, as in most state-produced excuses for killing people in war, the actual soldiers, their particular lives and concrete characteristics, are only important to the extent that they can be recruited into legitimacy-sustaining discourses. Margalit notes that Israel boasts

> a thriving industry of books dedicated to the memory of fallen soldiers. It was almost invariably pointed out that they secretly read the poetry of Rachel ("the Israeli Anna Akhmatova") or Alterman ("the Israeli Gumilov"). These soldiers never got much credit for their love of poetry while alive, only after their premature deaths.(p. 20)

I am reminded of the book my friend Phyllis showed me called *The Perfect War*, by James William Gibson, about the U.S. war in Vietnam. The author talks about the production of the image of the unknown soldier:

> The Pentagon, which waved its informal rules that 80% of a body must be recovered for it to be designated an Unknown, has now *intentionally destroyed all identification records related to the Unknown* to prevent inadvertent disclosure of information that might provide clues to the identity of the man intended to be a universal symbol of Vietnam battle dead. (p. 8; quoting *The New York Times*, May 29, 1984).

The Israeli government is certainly not alone in marshaling the resources of kitsch-in-uniform to deflect criticism, to forestall unpalatable questions from grieving families, to paste over the recurrent cracks in hegemonic, militarized, national identities. But they have raised kitsch-craft to new depths. In *In the Land of Israel* novelist Amos Oz finds both Israeli and Palestinian authorities working overtime to produce "that delightful weepy sensation" which cements identity in the bittersweet warmth of shared self-pity, self-congratulation, self-indulgence. (p. 165) Milan Kundera gives a wonderful explanation of kitsch in *The Unbearable Lightness of Being*:

> Kitsch causes two tears to flow in quick succession. The first tear says: How nice to see children running on the grass! The second tear says: How nice to be moved, together with all mankind, by children running on the grass!
>
> It is the second tear that makes kitsch kitsch.(p. 251)

Margalit calls the second tear a "meta tear" (p. 20)—the

glue holding together a state-orchestrated collective identity. The Israeli military/state apparatus cannot refrain from politicizing and administering the grief of soldiers because they want to control that second tear, the watershed that can either lubricate or dissolve a national identity.

April 21

PESSAH IS A very pleasant holiday, and a very long one. My *ulpan* is recessed for nearly three weeks, as are the children's schools. The kibbutz is full of guests, the pace is relaxed, there is lots of visiting with friends and relatives. The ever-present matzoh makes us (especially Oren) long for bread.

When we went to Yad Mordechai to see the facsimile of the battlefield there, Oren asked a lot of questions. I tried to explain about the invading Egyptian soldiers with tanks and planes, and the defending kibbutzniks with small arms at the top of the hill. The reenactment of the battlefield includes statues of the Egyptian soldiers, some tanks, and some models of armaments in the trenches of the kibbutz. Oren was fascinated, even thrilled, at the chance to get up on a tank, yet he was also a bit troubled by all the armaments, because he knows I dislike them. He wanted to know why there was a war. I said, with great trepidation, that there was a fight over whose land this was, the Jews wanted to stay on it and the Egyptians wanted to take it. Oren has the basic idea that defending yourself is okay, but taking from others is not. So he said, "The Jews were right, weren't they?" I said, hesitating, "yes, in this case they were right." How to explain to a five year old that, to the Arabs living there, the presence of the kibbutz was itself an invasion? Even worse, how to explain two thousand years of anti-Semitism, the desperate need for a Jewish homeland? Sometimes, confronted by the paradox of claiming for them an identity that much of the world despises, I question my conviction that my sons need to know their Israeli/Jewish heritage. They could take my Anglo-sounding last name instead of Gili's and melt into a Eurocentric mainstream, protected, perhaps, from direct assault. Someday I, and they, may regret my determination to connect them to their family and culture here.

Oren asked when the battle happened. "Was I born yet?" he asked. "No." "Were you born yet?" "No." "Was Memaw born yet?" "Yes." "Was she here?" "No, she lived in Indiana, far from the war." "It's a good thing she wasn't here," said Oren with conviction. "Because if she'd been here she might have been killed...and then you wouldn't have been born...and then I wouldn't have been born." How interesting to see a five year old coming to terms with the contingency of life.

And its tragedies. It was over a year ago that Oren asked me how my father died. I told him, and he said he wished he had enough magic to make my father come back to life. I thanked him for thinking of it, but I said I didn't think anyone had enough magic for that. He then asked if, after an old person dies, his spirit comes back in a baby. Oren invented reincarnation for himself! I told him I didn't know, that it's a possibility but no one really knows.

Katie, his little cousin in Indiana, told Oren that heaven is up in the sky. Oren doesn't know what to make of that, except he's sure that mice don't go to heaven (as in his book about Amos and Boris, when Amos the mouse contemplates his impending death and wonders if there will be mice in heaven) because how could a mouse get up in the sky?

The other day in the dining room Oren asked me if

my father was "an Indian, a white person, or a regular person?" "White," I answered. And "was HIS father an Indian, a white person, or a regular person?" "White," I replied. "TWO white people?!" Oren exclaimed. I ventured to ask what a "regular person" is. "Brown," said Oren. How interesting. What will Oren make of the fact that, in Hawaii, he is most definitely not considered a "regular person?" In Indiana, however, many people commented on how "brown" he is; compared to me and Ari, maybe; he looks very fair to me, but then I guess it all depends on what you compare him to. And also what is at stake. When my mother comments on how dark Gili's father is, and asks at the birth of both boys "are they dark?" I know what her agenda is.

Perhaps Oren's conviction that "regular people" are brown will help him to inhabit his whiteness on a slant, to mark whiteness as a problematic category with a troubled history rather than as an unremarkable norm. In the U.S. white is generally the unmarked category; when a newspaper story says "a person was shot" it is usually a white person who is referenced, who is taken to represent the universal human; other races are defined by some qualifying adjective. I remember the old crayon boxes in which a light pink/tan color was identified as "flesh." White people can think of themselves as having no color (colorless?). And when white is marked, it marks itself as superior. As a child I often heard people (white people, that is) say "That's mighty white of you," to commend an action, or "I'm free, white, and 21" to make a claim. How can I redefine racial identities to make a space for my children outside of these hegemonic constructions?

I remember Janet Gould commenting in her reflections about being a "mixed blood" (part Native American, part white) that we have uneven codes for naming race. "White" and "black" refer, in some general way, to skin color; "African-American," "Asian-American" and "Hispanic" anchor in location, in geography rather than biology. How would it change whiteness if we thought of it as Euro-American?

Oren and I once went to a nature workshop at the Bishop Museum on animal habitats. The young local woman teaching us about nature reproduced a modern western metaphysic with no questions asked, making an argument into a fact by familiarity and repetition. Her main point was to distinguish between "living" and "non-living" things: grass is living, soil is non-living; fish are living, water is non-living; moss is living, rocks are non-living. I told Oren afterwards that these are beliefs, not facts; I reminded him that many people, including the Indians, believe that grass, water and rock are living in their own way, that the earth is not inert matter. I told him that I think the Indians are right. He asked why, and we talked about the spirit of nature and life inhabiting all things. I am not sure what all this means to Oren, and I have faint stirrings of anxiety about the potential colonizing gesture at work in taking an indigenous metaphysics for my own. But it gives me a way into this cloudy area which I want my children to approach with openness and appreciation, not with arrogance or guilt. It gives western thinking a contingent status, makes it one way, not THE way. Perhaps it begins to deconstruct whiteness.

April 22

THE READING I am doing on Israel is very interesting. I hope some of the people I have written to respond soon, so I can begin to set up some meetings. There is so little in the way of a feminist presence on the kibbutz (the very phrase seems out of place) that I felt a great relief at reading the essays by women in Israel whose feminist politics are recognizable to me. I hope to meet the local Women in Black group soon. Sometimes I worry a bit about how such involvements will be taken here. How will the people of this kibbutz, who are generally so warm and welcoming to me, feel about a feminist peace activist in their midst? I suppose I have a cover of sorts, in that I can claim to be merely "studying" them. But I don't think that will last very long. I'm told there is one woman on the kibbutz who has some involvement in peace groups. Narkis mentioned her with a certain scorn, or at least amusement, in her voice. Which will be worse, being involved with women's peace groups or not shaving my legs?? Narkis invited me to join them in electrolysis of legs, underarms, and groin. I declined, trying desperately to get out of the conversation; it's clear that just letting hair grow on one's body is not an acceptable option. This is difficult because, at some level, I too worry about not being "feminine" enough with unshaved legs and armpits. I struggled with those fears two years ago when I stopped shaving (it was after my accident here, and my leg was in a cast for several months; the politics of personal hygiene was second to sheer discomfort). I guess I'll just ignore the problem, and trust in their basic politeness to accept it. Maybe I can survive in the category of "crazy (but likable) American feminist."

I rode one of the kibbutz horses today, a pretty gray part-Arabian who loves to run. It was a big event, getting back on a horse again after the last time I rode here, when I fell and broke my ankle. I rode cautiously, trying to let the familiar feel of a horse overcome the flutter of fear. The memory of that fall is vivid: the abrupt fear as the startled horse swerved suddenly, the loud crack of a bone breaking, the odd angle of my foot dangling off my leg, the hot sun and sand as I waited for help. The doctors put my leg "in traction" for a couple of days to get the swelling down. "Traction" consisted of putting my foot in a sock and tying the sock to a pole on the ceiling with some baling twine. Everyday they would "adjust" the traction by cutting and retying the twine, until it was too short to "adjust" any further. I wrote to my friend Cindy to send some more twine; I thought I had gotten the last piece!

The hospital workers were on strike during my stay, so I guess the conditions were worse than usual. I was told that conditions in the urban hospitals were more "modern" than in the rural hospital where I stayed. Narkis and Ofra, Gili's sisters, moved into my room to take care of me, taking turns sleeping there, washing me, bringing me medicine. For a while having some very strong pain killer as often as possible was my main concern, and no one on staff was about to bring it to me—you had to go get it yourself. People in the hospital without family or friends to care for them were shit out of luck—but the presence of family for those lucky enough to have them is probably better than the sterility of the more efficient hospitals.

I remember the team of "painters" who came to paint my room (while I was in it): paint a couple of swipes, argue endlessly over whether the colors of beige are exactly matching, take a 45 minute coffee break on the lanai outside my room, and begin again. At that rate, they are probably still "painting" the hospital. They always painted the places where people would be likely to lean, such as door frames; then everyone (nurses, doctors, guests) would lean against that spot and curse the paint that got on their clothes. I guess they don't have any "wet paint" signs in Ashkelon. My room was an unofficial corridor to the outside, and there was an ongoing parade past my bed; it was quite entertaining. I frequently saw cats run through the corridors; one day a dog came through my room. Never saw any chickens or camels, though, so it could be worse.

I shared a room with several other women, including a young Palestinian girl from Gaza, in for a very serious leg operation. Her mother stayed with her, sleeping on the floor sometimes, or sharing the bed. Unlike Narkis and Ofra, who boldly commandeered the supplies they needed to make a bed on the floor, she made do with very little. The doctors spoke to me more or less kindly in English, to the nurses in Hebrew, then to the girl's mother in a very sharp and accusatory Arabic. She spent a lot of time being self-effacing, conciliatory, and as invisible as possible so they would let her stay. Apparently she had been there a long time. I worried about what she had to eat, and tried to share my food with her. One day an Arab man came to visit, dressed in what looked to me like Bedouin clothing. For the occasion the girl and her mother covered themselves from head to foot. I, on the other hand, had just gotten out of surgery and felt totally miserable. It was hot, there was no air conditioning, I was in a lot of pain, and I just said to myself "fuck it," and lay there with as little covering as possible. Respect for cultural difference lost out to acute discomfort.

That must have been a hard time for the rest of the family. Oren had to be weaned then, and be without his *Ima* (mother) for a week. Gili had to take care of Oren, as well as worry about me. I was too out of it to even think about what the others were going through. Gili's family took such good care of me, even in the midst of all the relatives coming for Dov's 60th birthday party (which was why we were in Israel in the first place—and I missed the party after all). Then my parents worrying at home. What a lousy time for everyone. The only benefit was that I got closer to Ofra and Narkis.

Now, about Ari. He is such a joy. He is a happy

baby, always grinning his wide two-teeth smile, laughing a lot. Sometimes he looks so big to me, so long; other times he looks so little and vulnerable. He is beautiful, with big blue eyes. a wide forehead, and lovely shapely ears. Not much hair, though. People frequently comment on how gorgeous he is, and urge us to put him into a baby contest, or in TV commercials. (We gag at the thought, then wonder how much money it would bring.)

His children's house is a very amiable place, full of good-natured women and babies. Moms hurry in and out between their tasks in the kitchen; women with small children mostly work in the kitchen where they can leave frequently to go to their kids. (Dads do not—Gili and Alon, father of young Tami, are the only ones ever to venture in, except for birthday parties, when the whole family comes.) It is a light, airy, colorful place. The kibbutz really is a great place for children. I remember how, when I first took Ari to the children's house, I was worried. It was too uniform, all the children eating and sleeping at the same time. I felt like I was putting him in the army. I watched all the kids playing on the floor, slobbering on the toys others then played with, and I worried about germs, worried about giving offense, tried not to be predictably American, worried about germs. But now I love the place, its cheerful atmosphere and motherspace. Perhaps I just got used to it; there are no other options for child care. The kibbutz approach to raising children is far more regimented than we would like, sticking closely to feeding and sleeping schedules. But the emotional tone is so loving and cheerful that I can overlook the rest.

April 23

TODAY AS I left the house to go to the dining room for lunch, I saw a small lizard struggling up the walk. I don't know what to call these lizards; Dov calls them iguanas; they are medium sized, maybe 4-8 inches in length, and I see them often outdoors. I've often wondered why I don't see them indoors as well; I'm hoping my luck holds. In keeping with our friendliness toward geckos in Hawaii, Oren and I always say "hello lizard" and welcome them. This small one seemed to have trouble climbing over the sprinkler hose, so I moved it for him. Then I saw that he was dying. His belly was torn open, and he dragged his guts along behind him (why do I think it's a him?) as he struggled up the walk. Then, as I watched, he died. I heard myself say, in a voice that surprised me for the alarm it held, "What's wrong, honey?" I tried to help him into the shade under the steps, but by then I was only moving a corpse. I wondered guiltily if it was my fault, if somehow I had stepped on the little one, but unless he was already hurt he would have moved too quickly for that. I was embarrassed by the effect that small lizard's death had on me. Narkis, always quick to notice such things, pressed me on what was wrong, until I told her the story, embarrassed at the tears that wouldn't stay hidden. She laughed but also comforted me with a quick squeeze of her hand. I thought all day of that small lizard, its desperate efforts, the quiver in its body as it died.

There was a terrible story in the paper about a young woman shot to death by her brother-in-law over a quarrel concerning the family inheritance. Her husband, and the nine month old fetus inside her, also were killed. She was shot in bed, where she threw herself over the body of her one year old son to protect him from the bullets; a bullet caught the child's hand, which later had to be amputated. Only one year old, the child became, in that quick moment, crippled and orphaned. Who will love him now?

Perhaps death haunts me because I am worried about my mom, in the hospital for a week with an undiagnosed stomach ailment. Perhaps it is because there is always a simmering concern somewhere in my mind for my sons, and any death, even a small lizard, triggers that fear. I wear my gecko earrings for luck every time we leave the kibbutz, trying to ward off any encounters with the people and actions called "terrorist." I know in my head that the U.S. is a more violent society than Israel, that there is statistically greater likelihood of danger there; and, in fact, I feel a similar inchoate alarm there when my boys are away from me. As though my presence could protect them; perhaps I believe that because they do. But life a few kilometers from occupied Gaza has a sense of being in a war zone, despite the serenity of the kibbutz. The barbed wire coils along the kibbutz security fence, the ubiquitous armed soldiers, the frequent check points. . . the pervasive markers of war. In an indirect sense the kibbutz itself, its peaceful comfort, is a kind of marker of war; its safe and quiet life is constructed in contrast to the dangerous interruptions of the outside.

We went to Baruch and Ayala's tonight, sharing cake and coffee with these old friends of my husband's while the children played and the baby entertained us with giggles and coos. Ayala, a trim and businesslike woman, is former general secretary of the kibbutz, the elected leader; she and Gili and Baruch talk with animation about the kibbutz, how it has changed, whether for better or worse. She half scolds Gili for being out of touch with kibbutz life, for expecting it to be something it never really was even twenty years ago. Gili insists that the kibbutz has lost its ideological commitment, and explores ways to regain it. I wait through this discussion, peripherally interested, but eager to talk to Baruch about his time in the reserves. Finally the discussion breaks up and I get to speak with him.

I ask him what he does in the military; patrol Gaza, he replies, trying to bring some "law and order" to the place. How are you received, I ask. He says there is hostility from the adolescents and young people, that the children make a game of throwing pebbles, that the older people just go about their business. I fumble for questions to ask, to get at the tone and tenor of his presence there; how does he feel about it? Baruch, dear Baruch with his ready smile, gives me the straight party line about the occupation. The troops are merely keeping order, he says. The Arabs do a lot more violence to each other than we do to them, he says. It's not at all like Eastern Europe, where armed factions are killing children, he says. I venture to say that children are killed in the territories, too. "Not on purpose," he declares. Only, perhaps, during an encounter with a hostile crowd, when the necessary measures have to be taken and a child gets in the way. I remember Mariam Mar'i's account in *Jewish Women's Call for Peace* of a woman shot on her doorstep when she went out to help a small child who had fallen to a bullet there.(p. 17) But not in Baruch's world. Could he possibly believe what he is saying? Is he putting the best face on it for my benefit? He responds warmly to my inquiries, inviting me to ask more questions. Perhaps he is taking the role of public relations officer to this inquisitive American. "Most of the people in Gaza want peace," he declares. I imagine this is true; yet somehow I get the feeling he is saying it in order to isolate the rebellious ones, the "troublemakers." I ask about the women; Baruch talks about how primitive the Arabs are, how oppressed their women are; he contrasts them easily to the civilized west. I'm not used to hearing these words without quotation marks around them.

Baruch still engages me with his warm smile; he still reminds me of my father, his receding hairline topping a strong face and lively eyes. He is Gili's best friend from his days on the kibbutz, and I can see why. Where in his mind and heart does he keep the word "occupation"? "Oppression"? How does he separate his job so easily from injustice? I asked him if he thought the occupation had made Israeli society more violent, as many feminists claim. He says no, there was always a certain tendency in that direction; he gave the example of a man driving recklessly because, if he wasn't killed in the war, he believes he can flaunt fate on the road as well; but Baruch sees no difference now. No difference between wars that respond to external violence and a war that imposes it. No difference between defending against armies and policing civilians, between bullets coming from a uniformed enemy and stones thrown by another man's child.

There are so many grim stories in the paper, discretely revealed on the back pages of the *Jerusalem Post.* Three Arab youths (there are no Palestinians, it seems; only this amorphous group of "Arabs") are shot by undercover police as they sprayed graffiti on a wall. An Israeli couple, visiting a friend in this Arab village (this already marks them as liberals at least) witnesses the shooting and makes a complaint. Their Arab host is "badly beaten" for trying to intervene in the violence; the Israeli couple is charged with "insulting soldiers." None of these people have names. Why weren't the Israeli couple beaten? And what kind of crime is it to insult a soldier?

A Palestinian man living on the West Bank builds a house on his land outside his village, the second time in two years. And for the second time in that period, the Israeli authorities bulldoze the house. It seems that it is "illegal" because the area outside the village has been declared a "green zone." Sounds ecologically concerned, a gesture toward preservation of nature. Instead, it preserves the occupied territories for the Jews, whose expansion there is financed by the state. "This is the only land I own," says the man. His friends help him pull his belongings out of the house before it is demolished. His three children watch.

The *Jerusalem Post* is full of editorials ridiculing Bush for labeling settlement in the territories as an obstacle to peace. Who would have thought that I would find a reason to support the Gulf War President here in the Middle East?

April 24

THE WHOLE FAMILY went to Jerusalem on Saturday to show Simon and Lana around. When we got to the Wailing Wall (with characteristic insolence, Gili calls it the Whining Wall) we met the now familiar mix of tourists, believers, and soldiers. I was standing with the kids when a woman with a decided U.S. accent approached me and asked if I wanted to pray. The conversation switched quickly to English and she asked if I am Jewish. "No," I reply, knowing my answer will be unacceptable to her, "but my sons are half Jewish." Predictably, she dismisses this. "That's not possible," she claims. "You can't be a chicken and a bird at the same time." "A chicken is a bird," I jibe. The woman gives up on me and approaches my mother-in-law, opening her Bible, gesturing toward a page, and asking Batsheva why I did not convert to Judaism. I did not understand most of the ensuing conversation, but found out later that the woman wanted Batsheva to read a passage that asked forgiveness for allowing her son to marry a *goya*. Batsheva, bless her heart, shrugged her refusal and walked away. I sure married into the right family.

This incident evoked a smoldering resentment in me that comes somewhat as a surprise. What is at stake for me, that I keep attending to this woman's words? Perhaps it is because she represents the worst of the U.S. presence in Israel. The extreme Gush Emunim, the Kahane thugs, and other ultra-nationalist groups boast large numbers of immigrants from the U.S. in their membership. (So, of course, does the left, including feminism.) Or perhaps it is simply because her narrow-minded religious intolerance continues to irritate me. She personifies the arrogant pretensions of those who take the Bible to be a land granting institution and assume their faith is an infallible and total guide to life.

These explanations, while they ring true, don't quite address the lingering feeling of assault that stirs my resentments. I think the incident rankles because that woman, and the many like her, would deny my sons the link to this place that I claim for them. The secular laws of Israel recognize half Jews and allow them to be citizens; and coming from Hawaii, to be *hapa* (half one ethnicity, half another) is commonplace. (Although ironically my children are not viewed as *hapa* in Hawaii, because the category "Jew" is nearly invisible there, incorporated completely into the category of *haole*, or white person.) I claim a legitimate place for Oren and Ari in this vital, troubled land; it is one half of their heritage, one half of their stock of family, kin, community. I'm struggling to learn Hebrew to make it easier for them to do so, to give them at least a limited grounding in the language of their father and his people. Every holiday I try to teach the kids a bit more, to give them the cultural markers and practices that will make their Jewish side recognizable to them.

Sometimes this quest takes on comic proportions.

Gili is so thoroughly secular that he is no help at all in these endeavors. Last December I put together a Chanukah celebration, using a borrowed menorah and scrambling through Oren's books to find appropriate songs and recipes. When asked about Chanukah, Gili thought for a moment and said, "Well, you sing some songs, eat some food, that's about it." "Some songs?" I asked indignantly. "Could you be a bit more specific?" Under prodding, he called home and asked his sister. Unhelpfully, Narkis said "Well, you sing some songs, eat some food, that's about it." So we knitted together our familial version of the holiday, managed to have some decent latkes and kugel for dinner, and lit our menorrah in front of the Christmas tree.

Oren resides quite happily within his *hapa* status. He proclaims cheerfully to his friends that he is "half Christian and half Jewish." (I hesitate at the label "Christian," wondering if I can stretch it to be a broadly cultural, rather than religious, category. If Gili can be a secular Jew, can I be a secular Christian?) But *hapa*-ness plays differently in different contexts. When we lived in Indiana I took Oren to a nearby Methodist church to enroll him in their preschool, so he could meet some other kids and have a big indoor gym to play in on cold winter days. Like every other preschool we looked at, this one began each morning with a prayer and the Pledge of Allegiance. I did not want Oren forced into these rituals, which are quite foreign to him but heavily overcoded for me. So when the teacher asked us our religion, as part of the application process, I replied (a bit evasively) "His father is Jewish." The teacher immediately assured me that, while Oren needed to be quiet during the prayer and the pledge, he was not required to participate in either. (We left the relationship between being Jewish and objecting to the Pledge of Allegiance unexplored.) The warm and enthusiastic young woman in charge of the preschool was thrilled to have a

Jewish child in her class, and immediately invited me to do a Chanukah presentation for the children. ("Uh-oh," I thought to myself, "I'd better go do some research on Chanukah!") But in the end there was no need. . . the teacher called me the next morning, regretful and apologetic. The church fathers had ruled that no Jewish cultural or religious practices were allowed in the classroom. She reported quite frankly that, in the opinion of the men who run the church, exposure to religious differences at such an early age was unacceptably subversive. "We only have these kids a few hours a week," she explained, repeating what she had been told. "We don't want to dilute our message." I suggested that religious differences could be viewed with interest and appreciation rather than fear, but it was clear that she had been disciplined and saw no way out. Oren could attend the school, she explained carefully, but Jewishness could not.

The church fathers in Indiana are not so unlike the orthodox woman at the Wailing Wall. For the men, Oren was not acceptable because he was too Jewish; for the woman, he was not Jewish enough. Both had territory to protect. Neither could appreciate the rich opportunities that his *hapa*-ness provides, to cross cultural borders, to appreciate alternatives, to cherish the ironies and potencies of contrasting cultural practices.

There are different ways to do one's Jewishness. I do mine from the outside, so to speak. In Israel, in some ways I am a Jew. . . because, in the conflict with the Palestinians, it's clear which side I live with. Oren and Ari will come to their own terms with their *hapa* background, terms that I hope will contain affection and respect, along with a critical eye, for all the traditions they inhabit. But the woman at the Wailing Wall would deny them, and me, this room to negotiate. For her, Jewishness is not something you do, it's something you either are, or are not; a being, not a doing. Jewish identity is fragmenting all around her (the last time we were here, the heated debates about the status of some of the immigrants took place under the rubric "What is a Jew?") and my interlocuter is scrambling to put it back together, to make it one thing, to force me to do it "right," or not at all.

In *Storm from Paradise* Jonathan Boyarin talks about "the link between the given and the chosen" in his Jewishness. (p. xi) He finds a constitutive double consciousness in Jewish identity: first, because Jewishness has been defined for millennia by its rejection, and second, because there was an historical beginning, in the time of Abraham, for the Jewish people. Jewishness, then, has always been defined in relation to what it is not, and to what went before. Giving Jewishness a history, and naming its intimate relationship as Other to that which rejects it, can help to denaturalize it as a category. When an identity is given a context and a history, it is harder to endow it with a timeless and unchanging status. (Although the struggles to define that history and give meaning to that context can quickly become occupied by inflexible orthodoxies.) Boyarin finds in Jewishness "a model of an elaborately inscribed identity constructed in the awareness of difference." (p. 66) Viewing Jewishness as a complex encryption calls attention to Jewish identity as an act, a way of writing meaning onto life. Boyarin takes heart in the openings to otherness that a historically and relationally situated Jewishness can provide.

And so do I. When Oren was only a few days old I found myself fussing, much to the amusement of a Jewish colleague, about his future bar mitzvah. Looking back, the real focus of my concern was the larger question of negotiating his participation in Jewishness. A relationally, temporally defined Jewishness can make some room for Oren and Ari, offer some welcome on the borders of an identity terrain defined as permeable and shifting, not rigid and fixed. Of course they will ultimately have to negotiate that terrain for themselves, but Gili and I can either provide the resources to do so or withhold them, open doors or close them, sustain relationships or allow them to wither. My antagonist at the Wall would foreclose these negotiations before they begin, denying the contingent linkages and partial affirmations that my sons require.

April 25

IN MARCIA FRIEDMAN'S autobiography *Exile in the Promised Land* there is an account of a photo exhibit at the Israel Museum that lifted my spirits considerably. She writes:

> Oppression and violence became a way of life for a generation of Israeli men, but the Jews of Israel did not yet wish to recognize it. An exhibition of photographs at the Israel Museum broke through complacent denial, but only briefly and soon forgotten. Joel Kanter, an American immigrant, photographed the army at work in Gaza in a series of photographs entitled *Routine Check*, the army's term for the military units that patrolled Palestinian streets daily. The gallery was crowded with Israelis who filed slowly around the walls looking at pictures that revealed the terror on the faces of Palestinians as Israeli soldiers held billy clubs to their throats, pinned them to the ground with the heel of a boot on the back of a neck, shoved them against walls, guns

> in hand. The line of Israelis slowed down at the most violent of these pictures. Occasionally it stopped dead as crowds gathered around.
>
> "No one should have to see this," a woman shouted. "Why does the museum put these kinds of pictures on the walls?"
>
> "Everyone should have to see them. He's just showing us what we really look like."
>
> "It's ammunition for those who hate us."
>
> "It's the truth about ourselves."
>
> The arguments raged in the normally staid museum gallery, the still-hidden divisions, bitter and deep, exposed by this harsh view of the occupation. Juxtaposed with the photographs of the occupation were those of life on the kibbutz where Joel Kanter lived. The children in the photographs are robust and healthy. The old people, the first generation of pioneers, exude satisfaction. These pictures are full of flowers, alive with light. The contrast with the Israel of the occupation was stark, revealing the contradictions of life in Israel in the 1980s. (pp. 225-226)

And the 1990s as well. When I read this passage an enormous wave of relief broke over me. I'm not the first, I thought, I'm not the only one to love the kibbutz and hate the occupation. Of course I knew that already, knew that a full half of the people in this crazy country support some version of the left, would trade land for peace. But the political isolation I feel here, with only Gili to talk to frankly about politics, makes me forget.

April 26

TODAY IS *YOM HASHOA*, the day set aside for marking the anniversary of the Holocaust. I have a wild idea about writing a short story about a woman trying to write a short story about Israel and the Holocaust. She struggles with it because that is the forbidden analogy among Jews, especially with regard to Israeli foreign policy. Never compare anything that Israel does to the Holocaust, because it seems to paint Jews as Nazis and thus legitimizes their suffering at the hands of Nazis. But constantly invoke the Holocaust to defend Israeli policies and hold any criticism at bay. I want to write about this woman who sees a terrible inversion: in Europe, the camps held the horror, while the outside society went on as though everything were fine, normal. Here, inside Israel, everything goes on as though there were no occupation; it is outside, in the territories and beyond, that the oppression is felt and known and talked about. This woman wants to write about how the insides and outsides of things always leak, how the cost of not knowing what is there to know insinuates itself into the soul. But she also knows there are no ovens in the territories, no six million herded into camps, no soap made out of human fat, no lamps covered with human skin. But how much can this excuse? Is that the only standard of vice? If we don't make soap out of the Palestinians, anything short of that is acceptable? And who could "we" be here, for this woman, not an Arab, not a Jew, this intruder with her ready condemnations and the space to write these words?

April 28

RECENTLY AT LUNCH in the dining room I was introduced to a visitor, a woman who works in a shelter for battered women. She was talking about what the shelters do, the difficulty of providing adequate services. There are five in the country and, while it's a big victory to have them, she emphasized that it is not enough. A man sitting at our table said "Yes, that's a big problem among the..." My Hebrew wasn't good enough to figure out to whom he attributed wife-beating, but it certainly wasn't to his kind. The woman quickly disabused him of his self-satisfied view; no, she said, wife-beating crosses the lines he so confidently drew. Abused women, and abusive men, come from everywhere.

April 29

MORE CONTRADICTIONS, more doubleness. At 10:00 a.m. on Holocaust Day the sirens blew. The entire country came to a halt (at least, so they say; I'm not sure what the Palestinians and Israeli Arabs were doing). For two long minutes everyone stands still and remembers: remember the six million, one million children killed, gassed, burned, tortured; remember the indifference of the world to the horror; remember; remember; never again. I was in my *ulpan*, and I saw the tears in my friend Rosa's eyes matching my own. The wrenching photographs from the Yad Mordechai museum seemed imprinted on my retina, activated by the sirens and the silence. I knew that I was having exactly the response that I was supposed to have, but no political critique could short-circuit the searing imagery. I cried for the Jews, felt my fear and pain folded into theirs; I also cried for the communists, the gypsies, the trade unionists, the homosexuals—millions who were not Jews were killed; does anyone remember them? Or does only Jewish pain count? I cried for the people on the camp list in the museum at Yad Mordechai, for those with the same name as Gili's grandmother and great-grandmother. I cried for the despair of the women who tried to keep their children safe in a place dedicated to their death.

Yesterday's *Jerusalem Post* is filled with stories of Holocaust Day. There are memorials, marches, ceremonies, dedications, publications, interviews. A woman chosen to light a candle at one of the ceremonies, Sonya Lefkovitz, is one of only two women to survive Treblinka, to escape during the revolt; another, Ruth Elias, is a woman whose baby was killed at Auschwitz; again the tears come, this time I`m embarrassed, I'm in the dining room reading the paper and there's no moment of silence to legitimate this public display.

Then, I turn to the back page, where the paper carries news of the territories. Khalil Nader Hassan Hamisa, a 17 year old Palestinian, was shot and killed by the IDF. The gun he brandished at them was a toy, they discovered after the killing. Another young man, Jawad Khalil Asad Rahel, was also killed; the gun he pointed at them was real. What are those boys' mothers doing today, their fathers, their friends? How will they cope with the gaping hole in their lives? Will they fill it with more hatred, more intransigence?

Below appeared a small article on child abuse by concentration camp survivors' children toward their children, the third generation's legacy. Of the reported cases of child abuse in Israel, it says, 60% of the abusers are mothers, 40% are fathers. The accustomed gender linkage between abuse and men is interrupted; am I able to muster any tears for those mothers, since I seem to have so many available? No, the source dries up; I expect adults to perform miracles, to overcome their own legacy of abuse (the article says that the children of survivors often kept silent about their own abuse out of a need to protect their parents; but the third generation is far enough removed from the camps to be able to speak). If those mothers and fathers had gotten my attention when they were children, they would have received their fair share of these copious tears. Now I want to say to them, yes, you were hurt, but now you're hurting others; you have to stop. Israel is the child of survivors, abused and now abusing; how can a country of survivors break its chains? What reason is there to expect that a Palestinian state would be any different? Sometimes tears, produced earnestly or ironically, are the only response I can offer.

That night on the news, Holocaust memorial ceremonies are interrupted by an old man walking slowly down the street, leaning on a cane. He is wearing the striped camp uniform, including the small bowl-shaped hat. The on-the-scene television cameras zoom in on his face. He looks dazed, uncertain. His steps are slow. The announcer's voice identifies him as a survivor. He does not speak. A curious crowd gathers, a few tentative gestures are made to include the man, then he is whisked away. His is an unstaged presence, too raw, too ambiguous; it unsettles the careful orchestration of memory produced for public display. Within Holocaust kitsch, the specter of the Holocaust itself confuses and disturbs.

April 30

THE REPRESENTATIONS OF the Holocaust during these last few

days have been overwhelming, an onslaught of demanding, insistent, horrifying images. Of course Israelis are not talking, for the most part, about the *representation* of the Holocaust; they are simply talking about the Holocaust, as though it were a single thing, a straightforward truth to be told. *Shoa*, Holocaust, functions in Israel as an example of what Bakhtin calls the authoritative word. It resides in a distanced zone, its authority acknowledged in the past; it is the voice of the fathers. It is taken as a given, prior to anything that can be said about it. It demands acknowledgment, not by making persuasive arguments but simply by being. Its cultural authority predates our encounters with it. It is surrounded by taboos, and it can be profaned.

Shoa is the symbolic anchor of Zionism, a shorthand for the weight of world anti-Semitism, and the litmus test for political loyalty—peace demonstrators are frequently accused by hostile passers-by of forgetting the Holocaust. From it radiate a series of powerful demands: Never criticize a war while it is being fought. Always rally behind the cry of national security and accept it as the excuse for nearly any government policy. Never compare any act of Israel's with the Holocaust, but always equate Israel's opponents with the Nazis. Always emphasize the relative benevolence of the occupation, not the fact of it.

The authoritative word hosts numerous contradictions on its terrain. It shores up a siege mentality that justifies the investment of enormous national resources in the military, at the expense of schools, hospitals, and culture, while claiming the title "civilized" for itself and attributing barbarism to its enemies. The authoritative word provides the moral underpinnings for the Israeli authorities to represent themselves as omnipotent victors to the Palestinians in the territories, and as besieged victims to the rest of the world and to themselves.

The authoritative word resists reorientation. It does

not lend itself to revisions; its demands for allegiance are unconditional. It leaves little room for playing with the context of the word, or redrawing its borders; it is self-contained, indivisible. One can either affirm it or reject it, but it is difficult to make it one's own. Some Israelis approach the authoritative demands of the Holocaust by withholding rather than offering their fealty: a saying in Israel goes "There's no business like *shoa* business." My father-in-law responded to my questions about Holocaust Day with a shrug, commenting ambiguously "We Jews love to remember." A close friend confessed with considerable irony that he found himself in the bathroom taking a shit during the two minutes of national silence; he found it inconvenient to stand. When I asked him if I could write about the incident, he hesitated, then agreed, but requested anonymity. This passionately secular man knew that he was treading on hallowed ground. "After all," he said, self-consciously, "it IS the Holocaust."

One can either acknowledge or turn away from the claims on memory of the authoritative word, but it is difficult to rework those claims. Where in Israel is the effort to redefine the discourse, to revise its practices and put it into circulation differently? The challenge to state sponsored Holocaust kitsch is not cynicism, but redefinition; the challenge to official memories is not in forgetting, but in remembering differently.

Art Spiegelman's *Maus*, a set of comic books about the Holocaust, suggest ways to remember differently. He tells the story of his father's life in Poland before the war, his increasingly desperate efforts to protect himself and his family, his deportation to Auschwitz, his survival. The Jews are portrayed as mice, the Nazis as cats, the Poles as pigs. The juxtaposition of the usual associations of comics with the trivial, and the Holocaust with the epic, provides the space within which he does his work. While he tells his father's story, he also tells about the telling, bringing the act of representation into the story. He locates his own resentments and obsessions alongside those of his father, sometimes imagining himself the victim and his parents the murderers, while highlighting the irony of such self-preoccupation. Spiegelman portrays the horrors starkly, but does not canonize the victims—his father turns out to be manipulative, domineering, rather unlikable. The author's own relation to the Holocaust, as a Jewish writer making a living from the onslaught on the Jews, occasions ironic comment: at one point he draws himself writing on a desk supported by piles of little mice skulls.

Maus remembers, but it insists on attention to *how* one remembers. I wonder what would happen if each locality in Israel were left to make Holocaust Day in its own way, to come to active terms with it, not just be carried by state definitions of history? Bakhtin says that the authoritative word is always calcified, offering no space for play, no contradictory emotions or cacophonous internal space. But perhaps the agents of the central order work so hard at maintaining the official definition precisely to ward off pending recalibrations of the demands of memory on life.

May 1

Los Angeles is burning, the aftermath of the acquittal of the white police officers accused of beating Rodney King. At night we watch the news on Narkis's television, and try to answer people's questions here about it. I try to talk about institutionalized racism, the legacy of slavery, the unresponsiveness of the political system, the complacency of whites.

In my limited Hebrew, the words sound simplistic; in English, even to my own ears, it sounds too abstract, too unconnected to the raw events on the screen. Our kibbutz friends are incredulous—"How could this happen in America?" Funny how other people's hatreds and obsessions seem transparently unnecessary, while one's own seem complex and insurmountable. Aviv, Gili's brother-in-law, is open to considering racism in the U.S. but resistant to any parallels to his home. Dov genuinely wants to hear my ideas: I remind him of how familiar the riots are, reminiscent of Newark, Detroit and Watts in the late 60s, New York in the 1920s; that most Americans have little historical memory and are taken by surprise at the eternal recurrence of the same old hatreds. Dov asks if I think it is the same in Israel, with the Palestinians; of course it is not exactly the same, but the parallels are there so I nod, grateful that he is willing even to think such thoughts.

May 2

THE HEAVY RAINS last winter have produced an unbelievable wealth of wild flowers. Today we visited a huge field of bright red poppies. They covered acres of pasture, rippling over gentle hills, a magnificent crimson sea on a background of vivid green. People come from all around the area to play, as we did, on the rich red carpet of flowers.

May 6

TODAY IS *YOM ZIKAREN*, Memorial Day, dedicated to the memory of the over 17,000 soldiers killed in Israel's wars since the founding. Memorial Day looks backwards, mourning the fallen. Last night there was a ceremony on the kibbutz, today one at the *ulpan*, both accompanied by the nation-wide sirens signaling a minute of silence, remembering. I stood last night with my arms around Oren, thinking please, no more wars, not for my sons, not for these children, no more killing. Would Israel's self-understanding shift if it could redefine the remembering more toward the future, toward a determination to avoid more death rather than a commitment to avenge past deaths? Did anyone else perform a silent revision, warding off future loss instead of acknowledging that from the past?

What selective memories are honored in this country of heroes and martyrs, knit together with blood and history. Everywhere there are memorials, ceremonies, official and unofficial rituals that define the past, capture it within the cruel and tragic boundaries of Israeli kitsch. Israel's kitsch, their categorical agreement with being, underwrites a militarized self-understanding. Heroes, martyrs, victims; suffering, persecution, survival. It is a gendered kitsch, with heroes and warriors occupying the masculine pole while victims carry the feminine. The hegemonic Israeli self-understanding is thoroughly masculine, the proud and manly warrior prepared to die for his country.

In Avishai Margalit's discussion of the "should soldiers cry" debate, he misses the gendered dimension of its kitsch. Everything about tears that the *sabra* disdains is coded feminine: helplessness, vulnerability, passivity, openness to others, grief in the face of loss. The prized "take-charge" mentality of the *sabra* is both a gung-ho masculinity and a strong-man resignation. The archetypic *sabra* soldier is eager to do what's necessary, regretful of its costs, yet proud to pay the price exacted. Marcia Freedman comments that in the schools Israeli children learn, as a maxim, the words of a famous Israeli warrior, "It is good to die for one's country." Aaron Wolf's account of his time in the Israeli army stresses the hero status accorded to soldiers by school children; he and his friends all wanted to be pilots or paratroopers. (The girls cannot become pilots or paratroopers; do they dream instead of marrying them?) Gili says that as children they referred to Jews who would not defend themselves, contemptuously, as "soap." It is not a discourse that fields many openings for critical reflections on patriarchy, war, or racism.

The military inscribes itself on physical, social and bodily landscapes in myriad ways. The ubiquitous brown uniforms on young bodies, machine guns swinging from shoulders, seem to inhabit every street, bus stop, restaurant. Military training writes itself on bodies, on their carriage and musculature, in a particularly public way in a society in which nearly every Jew has been or will be a soldier. In *A Purity of Arms* Aaron Wolf recalls the identifiable bodily markings left by paratrooper training:

> Repeated jumps from the Eichmann [a training tower] leave a paratroop trainee with burn scars along his neck that give me a certain amount of prestige in Israel, where everyone knows what they mean. When I hitchhike to the kibbutz on weekends, people who pick me up, seeing the burn marks, say respectfully, 'Oh. Paratoop training, eh?!' I am supposed to think of the burn marks as a badge of honor." (p. 191)

The symbolic significance of the characteristic burn marks has completely replaced their functional meaning, since the Israeli military no longer uses parachute jumps in combat. (They have been replaced by the more precise operations of transport helicopters. (p. 201)) But the bodily markings of military prowess continue to provoke the admiration of school children and the respect of adults, and to underwrite a militarized, implicitly masculinized, notion of citizenship.

Both "Arabs" and "women" are folded neatly into the metaphoric apparatus privileging Jewish, military, masculinity. "Women" (that is, Jewish women) take up necessary supporting roles: the plucky female officer; the loving wife back home; the devoted mother raising her children to be soldiers. They are coded feminine, positive; lesser than men, but crucial and highly valued in their place. Not so dissimilarly, the representational practices creating "Arabs" also work the feminine side of the street. "The Arabs" are weak, stupid, not a worthy enemy but a sneaky and therefore dangerous one. "The Arabs" are a mystery, ruled by dangerous primal forces, inscrutable, disloyal to civilization. The Arabs play the woman to Israel's man, a deadly affair. They are coded feminine, negative; lesser than Jews, stirring both fear and contempt, yet in their own way necessary to the maintenance of hegemonic Jewish self-understanding. Could the widespread contempt for "the Arabs," manifested frequently and casually even among my Labor party friends who support "land for peace," could it be a kind of self-contempt, a disdain for those who allow themselves to lose?

In *Keepers of the History* Elise Young finds a consistent intertwining of "Arab" and "feminine." She recounts a terrible incident on May 20, 1990: a group of Palestinians from Gaza are waiting at Rishon Lezion, a place outside Tel Aviv from which day labor can be arranged (commonly known as a slave market). A young Israeli man in army fatigues, carrying an automatic weapon, asks to see their identity cards. As the men offer the required cards, the Israeli opens fire, killing seven and wounding ten more. The media reports: "one Israeli driving by stops his car, jumps out, and dances around their bodies." (p. 1) The media further reports "that the murderer is himself a victim—of unrequited love. He told his girlfriend that if she would not take him back, he would go out and kill. Palestinians and women became confused in his mind." (p. 2)

Young goes on to analyze women as an occupied territory, conflating Palestinian and feminine from the opposite political direction, with the intent of valorizing them as parallel victims. It is hard to know precisely what to make of this semiotic intersection of race and sex (Jew is to masculine as Arab is to feminine) when it is put to work by the killers as well as the defenders of the weak. The metaphors become even more slippery when complicated by the history of anti-Semitism, where it is the Jew who is feminized, othered, construed as irrational, dirty, and sinful, while the Christian passes as the implicitly masculine universal norm, the fully human "man."

And the kibbutz is such pleasant, welcoming place, a lovely home. The physical and social landscape—the slope of carefully tended lawns, the unevenness of the walking path near our house, the good-natured buzz of conversation in the dining room—is familiar and dear. I love Ari's *beit tinnokot* (infant's house); the mothers gather at noon to feed the children, and we laugh together and admire each other's babies. We tell our birth stories, marveling at each other's courage or luck, savoring the details of this one's rapid one-hour delivery, another's 20-hour struggle. The air rings with good humor and love, in three languages—English to accommodate me, Spanish from those native to South America, the guttural Hebrew this land demands. At these moments, and there are many, I love the kibbutz, love its warmth and beauty. I feel disloyal to the fine people here, many of whom would find the currents of my thoughts distasteful, my reservations arrogant or uninformed.

Tomorrow is *Yom Hatzmaut*, Independence Day.

The kibbutz is preparing for the holiday, which involves a trip to a military air base for an air show (Oren is delighted) and to the beach. Everywhere there are Israeli flags, flapping blue and white in the wind. We even have a string of them for our front porch. My friend Jana tells me it is a wonderful holiday, that everyone is happy. Everyone? I wonder. Are the one million Israeli Arabs happy? How about the Palestinians from the territories? It is close to treason to even entertain these questions here.

May 8

THE INDEPENDENCE DAY celebrations were all they promised to be. Memorial Day came to an end in the evening, with a solemn ceremony at which the flags were taken from their half-mast position, where they had been for the remembrance, and raised to full height. The mood abruptly broke, shaking off the melancholy of the day of mourning and switching into a celebratory mode. There were songs, readings, dancing. Oren's class from the *gan* (kindergarten) danced, and we were so proud of Oren. At first he didn't want to participate, but he didn't seem truly anxious about it so I talked him into it. He seemed to have a good time doing it, and he knew the whole dance very well. He got to wear blue and white streamers on his wrists that made a very satisfying noise as they rustled. Afterwards he seemed quite proud of himself. It was wonderful for Gili to see his son taking part in the kibbutz ceremonies, to feel his son at home in the place that is still, after everything, his home.

Then there was dinner, festive and crowded with visitors. Afterwards the dancing began outside under the flags and lights. It was delightful to watch the energetic folk dances, to see people of all ages dancing together. Even the teenagers took part in the evening, staying carefully to the side to preserve their separate identities but there nonetheless. The integration of people of all ages into this community is impressive—there is little segregation of the old or the young. People milled around, greeting each other, admiring babies (Ari got more than his share of attention), sipping coffee or punch.

Thursday we went to the air force base. There was no "air show" as I understand them, in the sense that the planes did not "perform" in the air. Instead, the planes were carefully displayed, along with tanks, anti-aircraft weapons, helicopters, and other armaments. These shows take place at air force bases all over Israel. Thousands of people attend these displays of military might, to admire the weapons and read about their killing capacity. It is the Israeli thing to do on Independence Day.

I strive to demilitarize this display for Oren, to facilitate his fascination with airplanes and helicopters in some context other than war. We count the wheels and propeller blades on each plane, look to see how many people it can hold. My heart sinks when Oren asks about "the rockets" (bombs). I tell him what they are for, but try to direct his attention toward other things. He asks if the bombs are still used. I say that I hope not, that I hope there are no more wars. He agrees, and says "If you drop a bomb on a house, the house would explode, and the people inside would explode unless they weren't there." I wonder what "explode" means to him, wonder if my attempt to demilitarize his life is the right thing to do. I can't let militarism and violence become ordinary for him; I want it to be strange, horrifying, to require an explanation rather than fit into the natural order of things. I don't want him to develop the capacity to become hardened to it; yet I don't want to traumatize him either. I feel that I am waging a one-woman struggle against the constraints of manhood, trying to find ways to raise a boy to be a man that don't embrace the foundational norms of violence, separation, and contempt for the weak. I know there are other mothers doing it, but there is no public context to support it, so it feels like an isolated endeavor. Especially here, in this country so embedded in its warrior identity. I would not want to raise my sons in Israel.

As we walk back to the bus I have a brief conversation with Calanit, one of the office workers in the kibbutz factory. Smoking one cigarette after another, she speaks about her reservations: "We teach the children how to kill." "They so admire the soldiers, they want to be like them." She shakes her head, regretful at the paucity of opportunities to imagine a different future. "It is our life," she says, with what looks to me like fear in her eyes. (I learn later from Gili that one of her sons is about to go into the military for his obligatory three-year term. Then I understand that flash of fear, the emotional charge in her voice.) I venture to suggest that it could change. "Not in our lifetime," she says, with resignation, firmly. "There are too many differences." Calanit's mother-fear could be a grounds for opposition to this intransigent militarized state; her resignation undercuts that possibility, reestablishes the military priorities against a backdrop of regret.

The crowds at the air base are an impressive cross-section of Israel's population. Jews come in all colors. The European features and coloring of the Ashkenazi Jews is intersected by the darker colors and hair of the Sephardim, the blackness of the Ethiopian Jews, even the occasional Asian face. Jewish identity is hard to pin down within the prevailing categories of understanding, at least those that I know: it is a race, yet it is not tied to color; it is tied to nationality, yet Jews all over the world who are not Israeli would probably put their loyalty to their country of citizenship ahead of any allegiance to the state of Israel; it is connected to religion, yet many Jews are thoroughly secular. Looking at the panoply of colors, features, textures, languages, I wonder how the dichotomy between Arab and Jew can be sustained in the face of all the diversity on both sides of the slash. What about the Jews from Arab countries? The Arabs from Israel? What about their common Semitic background, their shared history of rejection by European imperial officials as "primitive" and "backward"? In *My Enemy, My Self* Jewish writer Yoram Binur talks about how easy it was for him to pass as an Arab, a matter of clothing, accessories, and body language. (And spoken language too, of course; Binur was fluent in Arabic.) "The moment they [other Jews] saw me with an Arabic newspaper and wearing ragged clothes, I was an Arab as far as they were concerned." (p. 211) Among Palestinians, proper participation in the "elaborate customs and etiquette" by which individuals established their relationships gained him admittance.(p. 212) If "Arab" and "Jew" are such porous and unstable unities, why doesn't the leakage in each category undermine the hostility between them?

I often hear Israeli Jews say that the Jews must have Israel because they have no where else to go, while "the Arabs" have a lot of countries and could go elsewhere. Unpacking this claim leads into a morass of fears and defenses. In a country of immigrants, many of the Jews certainly did have somewhere else to go; they could have stayed in their country of origin. Saying they have nowhere else to go is really a way of saying that there is nowhere else in the world where it is safe for Jews, where they can live without fear of the next pogrom, the next round of persecution. But how safe is it really to live in a country with a perpetually hostile occupied population next door? How safe is it to live without peace?

Similarly, "the Arabs" are not a homogenous group with a uniform claim to citizenship in other lands. Palestinian Arabs have lived on this land, Palestine/Israel, for a long, long time. Why is their claim to the language of exile and homelessness not honored? Israeli citizenship categories are generous toward Jews, welcoming virtually any Jew from anywhere. But no Arabs are so included, even if their families lived on what is now Israeli land for generations. Palestinian labor in low income occupations is (warily) welcome—but not their citizenship. The right of return is zealously preserved for some, ruthlessly denied to others. Meanwhile, Palestinians are not welcomed *en masse* in Jordan, Egypt, Iraq, or Syria; they are foreigners there too. Israeli insistence on this category of "Arabs" is a way of ignoring national and religious differences within the Arab world, of pretending that they are all the same and therefore that the Palestinians have other possible homes.

On Israeli soil there is a memorial, built by the Egyptian government as a part of the Camp David Accords, to the Egyptian soldiers killed in the wars against Israel. We went there soon after arriving on the kibbutz, read the solemn inscriptions in several languages on the phallic marble monument. In some ways this memorial breaks down the dualism of Arab and Jew by marking Arab deaths as worthy of remembrance and mourning. This marker interrupts the dominant discursive terrain upon which memory is constituted by claiming a place there for The Enemy. Yet in another way this memorial sustains that discourse in that it keeps the politics of memory production tightly wrapped around the figures of "the fallen." The heroes and martyrs of war (not its civilian victims, not those who resisted, certainly not those who opposed the wars) are the central representations of the past. The patterns of national memory close in ruthlessly on the figure of the warrior, then make a minor accommodation to include (some) enemy warriors as well. It is a miserly discourse, offering few openings to imagine, perhaps, a hero who is not a warrior, or even a person who is not a hero and only wants to live.

May 9

MUCH TO OREN'S delight, today is *Lag Ba'omer*, a children's holiday, loosely translated by Gili as Robin Hood Day. I'm not clear on the historical significance of the event, but each child goes to the *gan* (kindergarten) with his or her own bow and arrows. The children get to ride behind Aviv's tractor down past the orchards to the *bustan*, a shaded grassy area where they can build a bonfire and have a picnic.

It is so rewarding to see Oren become part of the *gan*. He brandished his bow and arrows proudly this morning, showing them to his friends. His Hebrew grows by leaps and bounds, in stark contrast to my own laborious efforts. Sometimes the rougher children intimidate him, but his cousins try to intercede. He loves to visit Narkis's house, to play with her boys and watch their Robin Hood video in Hebrew. He is becoming friends with his cousins, and affectionate toward his grandparents, aunts and uncles. He still misses his pal Emma in Hawaii, and his cousins Katie and Tyler in Indiana, but the roots of his belonging here have been planted.

May 10

GILI'S FAMILY CAME over for pancakes (my culinary specialty around here) this morning. They asked, tentatively, if we are thinking about staying in Israel permanently. I remark that I would not want to be so far away from my mother, especially since her health is not good. This response, while true, is also a cover for hiding my aversion to raising my sons in such a militaristic environment (although, if we went back to Indiana to my family, it would not be altogether different there). Eventually I ventured to raise my fears about the military, and Gili's parents nod their understanding. They are not surprised, only regretful.

The more Gili and I reflect on this possibility for our future, the more my ambivalence grows. In some ways there would be no greater gift to Oren and Ari—to live in this warm and secure place, with loving, vital grandparents, aunts, uncles and cousins, to grow up in the midst of such a passionate and good-humored community. I would eventually get used to the things that agitate me now. After all, I got used to the children's house, which first seemed so regimented, and now is comfortable. To "get used to" means to incorporate that which is initially strange into the familiar frame of habit, to cease to see it as requiring an explanation and simply accept it as the way things are. I hear an invitation issuing to me from within Israeli kitsch, an ambiguous opportunity. I can imagine myself in ten or fifteen years, seeing my boys off to wars I still detest, folding my opposition into a discourse of necessity and regret. The image stirs a wave of anxiety, a restless fear; almost as much as I fear for my sons, I fear for myself.

May 11

TODAY AT THE *ulpan* we were treated to a pantomime about life in Israel. Our teacher explained it as the *maagal hiyeem*, the circle of life. It began with a *brit mila* (circumcision), then a *bar mitzvah*, then the army, then marriage, then fatherhood. Presented by a couple from a local kibbutz, the show was lively and entertaining. It poked fun at the cockiness and ineptitude of a young soldier in basic training, followed by his silly, semihysterical mother, with her absurd turban, flapping shopping bags, and foolish facial expressions. There were two women in the story: the sweetheart wooed by the soldier, and the frantic, ridiculous mother running after her new soldier/son with bags of sandwiches. Smadar, our teacher, emphasized that it represents the unique life cycle in Israel, because the combination of Jewishness and mandatory army service marks life here as different than other places. Still, I wonder how an exclusively male set of experiences get made into THE life cycle. Women share some points of this cycle, but their take on it is absent; there are babies, but no birth, or menses, or lactation; there is a mother, but no mothering beyond the idiotic woman with the turban and the sandwiches. Certainly nothing about being *bat mitzvahed* into a religion that marks you as inferior, or about going into the army only to find yourself working clerical jobs, subordinate to men.

The pantomime was well received by its audience, students glad for a break from the classroom and ready for a bit of entertainment. It was not meant to be a sociological treatise on life in Israel, nor to sustain the kind of criticism I am applying. But I could not help but see it as another manifestation of an officially endorsed set of identity practices. It charms us while recruiting us further into the prevailing naturalization of conventional gender arrangements and of a society organized around war. The *ulpan* is the institutional vehicle the Israeli state has created to introduce the *olim hadashim* into Israeli society, to make new Israelis. It takes this motley assortment of Russians, Africans, Europeans, British, North and South Americans, the occasional Asian, and tries to shape a set of common experiences to anchor a new national identity. The *ulpan* takes what literary critic Homi Bhabha calls "the shreds and patches of cultural signification" and knits them into "the certainties of a nationalist pedagogy." (p. 294). There is little explicit propaganda involved; it is a more subtle and robust process of creating a shared national narrative. The parameters of the story are dependably patriarchal and militaristic. The pantomime is just one small repetition of these themes: the image of the mother rides upon the familiar stereotype of the "Jewish mother"; her anxiety over her son's entry into the military is mocked by her silly turban, her shopping bags, her comic portrayal of the concerns of motherhood. The pantomime was an exercise in containing maternal concern, overdoing it and thus deflecting its power into absurdity. One hears the son say "oh, Mom."

It is a stark contrast to the anxiety of our friend Geula over her two small sons. We stood in front of the kibbutz dining room one evening, watched our kids play in the twilight, and spoke about the military. She recognized my discomfort with the Independence Day air show and its the celebration of killing machines. "I know," Geula said. "When I came here from Brazil I felt the same way." But she has resigned herself to the constant military presence, seeing it as an unfortunate necessity. Still her voice broke when she spoke of her little boys, their future military duty: "I could die when I think of them." Omer, her husband, has suggested to their three year old that he could be a musician in the army, presumably avoiding combat. "On no," the child replies. "I want to be a soldier." "What can I do?" Geula demanded. "It is our life."

My timid suggestions that the military may be necessary, but that there is a difference between regretting it and celebrating it, go nowhere. And in the end, maybe her tragic stance is not so different from the comic woman with the turban: each one derails and deflects the potential politics of mothering—the need to create a safer world, to protect the weak, to communicate rather than fight—one by caricature, the other by resignation. "It is our life."

May 12

TODAY I WENT on the bus to Beer Sheva, to the university there, for a seminar on gender and writing. Looking at the dusty beauty of the countryside in central/southern Israel, I see the occasional building standing abandoned and isolated in a carefully cultivated field. Was this the home of a Palestinian family who "left" in 1948? The standard Jewish/Israeli account of these empty buildings is that their owners "left." As though they voluntarily got on a bus and left town for greener pastures. No mention of civil war, of home and exile.

Soon after our arrival on the kibbutz we went on a hike conducted by the unofficial kibbutz historian, a serious man with a careful knowledge of and love for this land. It was a terribly hot afternoon, with a merciless *jamsin* (desert wind) blowing from the Negev. We worried about the sun burning down on Ari's tender baby skin. All the adults carried large canteens and coolers, offering water frequently to the children. We walked through the cattle pastures, across the hills to the highest point in the area, once used by the ancient Hebrews to build bonfires signaling to neighboring villages the much celebrated birth of a boy. History speaks to us as we cross these ancient hills...and yet history is also silent. We come to some very old ruins of buildings; no one knows what they are. Gili recalls similar trips in his youth through the area surrounding the kibbutz, hiking through ruins he now recognizes as abandoned Arab villages. He remembers wondering, as a child, who lived in those houses, but he never asked. "Why not?" I asked him. "I don't know," came his unsettled reply.

I can see why it would never occur to a kibbutz child to ask such a question. The schools, the military, the state, the press, all orchestrate a deafening silence about such inquiries. The Arabs simply "left." Israeli society works actively at forgetting. A few years ago, the bulldozers came to demolish the ruins Gili recalls from his youthful camping trips, lest any Palestinians try to claim their former land (or any inquisitive Jewish child ask forbidden questions).

The complex politics of legitimized memory and orchestrated forgetting haunt Israel in ways difficult to unwind, immersed in the difficult relationship of time to power. Nietzsche counseled forgetting rather than memory because he feared the politics of resentment, the endless detailed recall of one's own victimization that is so often mean-spirited and self-defeating. One savors one's weaknesses, redefining them as virtues. An active forgetting of one's own grievances might prompt a greater generosity toward others. It might also leave one's own group open to further violations. Hegel insisted on remembering because he thought eventually one could put all the information together into a complete, whole picture, a universal truth. But if all efforts at understanding the power of the past in the present are partial, rooted in someone's perspective rather than a God's-eye point of view, then no completed picture is available. Jonathan Boyarin recommends a welcome double gesture toward the past, one that recognizes both the familiar and the distant: "We need constantly to be interrogating and recuperating the past, without pretending for long that we can recoup its plenitude." (p. xvi) Such a double gesture might enable Israeli

Jews to recalibrate their memory practices toward some inclusion of the stories the Palestinians tell. Memory and forgetting turn out to be, not direct opposites, but uneasy partners, their incompatibilities folded into their mutual dependencies. Forgetting is not simply the absence of memory; it has its own presence, in the unspoken weight in one's heart, and the unheeded recollections of others. Memory, similarly, is more than a straightforward presence; it is both an inexhaustible resource and a selective account. Memory and forgetting are mined opportunistically by the Israeli state, to feature Jewish victimization and excuse Israeli power. Palestinians and Jews alike might find it more difficult to be swept away by their own memories if they recognized the forgetting required to do so.

I'm pleased that Smadar (my teacher) mentioned the existence of Israeli Arabs the other day in class. She noted Israel's frequent wars, people's longing for peace; she said several times "there are one million Arabs in Israel. They live here too; they've been here a long time." She also mentioned the Arabs in the occupied territories. She made it clear that she disagrees with the "throw them out" ideology of the right. I was oddly comforted by her modest gestures in class toward the recognition of the humanity of the Palestinians—comforted because I hear so little of it, and because at least this group of *olim hadashim* has been reminded that "the Arabs" live here too.

May 13

I MET SOME fascinating women in Beer Shiva yesterday. Elena Loory, from Women's Studies and History, talked about the effect of the rabbinical courts on women's lives. Women have no standing as witnesses there, so if a divorce case goes to the religious courts the woman is doomed. There is a parallel set of civil courts which are less unfriendly to women, but the religious right is pushing for more family matters to be delegated to the rabbinical authorities. The growing power of the religious courts seems to reflect a "deal" between secular men and Orthodox men, at women's expense; the religious establishment agrees to support the governing coalition in exchange for considerable control over personal and family life, especially over the lives and bodies of women. The religious courts allow bigamy (for men, of course); the first wife is supposed to agree to the arrangement, but a petition signed by 100 rabbis can overrule her opposition. A husband can get custody of his sons over age six in order to see to their religious education. The wife has few acknowledged grounds to make her case. In *Keepers of the History* Elise Young also discusses the power of the rabbinical courts over women. The courts maintain a blacklist of several thousand women who are prohibited from legally marrying, usually because they or their mothers are rumored to have committed adultery. (p. 170) Elena also talked about the orthodox Jewish influence on education: more conventional gender stereotypes in textbooks, more attention to boys in the classroom.

Niza Yanay is another very interesting woman at the university there. She teaches social psychology and women's studies, lives on a nearby kibbutz. I liked her at once; she has red hair and lively, intense eyes. She is doing some fascinating research on racism among adolescent religious girls. National surveys have found that, among Jewish adolescents, secular girls are the most tolerant toward Arabs; secular boys are the next most open-minded group; religious boys the next, and religious girls the least tolerant. This is fascinating; the first two categories are what one would expect, given conventional gender arrangements; but the second two are a reversal of the expected. Why are the religious girls more racist than the boys? She and a student are doing research in the schools, interviewing religious girls, to try and find out why. I thought immediately of a psychoanalytic explanation, some sort of sexual fear, but that may be too obvious and superficial (or maybe too obvious and deep). I want to hear more about her work.

I had lunch with Phyllis Lassner, the woman who gave the talk (a visiting professor from the University of Michigan—she speaks no Hebrew, so maybe there's hope for me!); her husband; Elena; an interesting woman named Carol; and Carol's elderly father-in-law. I liked the old man's strong, patient face; he and I greeted each other, then he lapsed into amiable silence. I regretted that he was excluded from the conversation, but I couldn't think of a way to draw him in without interrupting the flow of things, and I was not close enough to him to begin to speak on our own. When Carol brought him hot water, but no tea bag, he remarked "just like the old country." Carol said the old country is Poland.

I wish I could have spoken with the old man. He represents for me a dimension of Jewish culture that I see little of in my corner of Israel, the East European *shehtl* Our kibbutz works up more passion about soccer matches than they do about *Yiddishkayt.* I wonder what the old man makes of the brash *sabra* youth, what he would say about the "should soldiers cry" debates. Is he transplanted or uprooted? Is he at home?

The women asked me about my work, and I began with hesitation to talk about this journal. As I spoke, I began to figure out that the journal format is congenial to me because I am feeling my way through a very complex set of practices, events and histories, and while I have some strong feelings about them, hopefully some insights into them, I have no final conclusions to offer. Conventional academic writing crowds out both the personal and the tentative; it requires firm arguments and clear resolutions; it stands at an unambiguous distance from its material. I have no neat narrative to tie up the loose ends here, no clear whole within which to subsume the fragments. The available narrative strategies are part of the problem; the stories of Jewish resistance to Arab attacks and world indifference, or Palestinian resistance to Israeli repression and world indifference, or careful academic evenhandedness in the face of the intransigence of others—each of these arrangements of the story takes its place in the fixed landscape of available "positions" on the "Arab-Israeli conflict." It is this fixity that needs disturbing. But the I/i/eye writing this is not outside these narrative strategies, nor outside of the persistent demand for some overarching account of things. I turn to this kind of writing in the hope of creating a space to think against, perhaps even outside of, the prevailing curtailments of understanding.

The risks involved seem considerable: the risk of being dismissed in intellectual circles for sentimentality and lack of rigor, in political circles for the absence of a clear agenda of action. The risk of offending people I love. The risk of self-indulgence. Once you begin to crack the facade of impersonality in writing, how to avoid the scenario in which Everything That Happens To Me Is Incredibly Important And The World Needs To Hear About It? The risk of self-scrutiny becoming confessional, so that a move against power (of the dominant narratives) becomes reincorporated into power (of the judging gaze).

These fears are endless. Yet the possibilities beckon—to write against the grain of the established accounts, and against the processes by which they become established, and thus to open up space for a different account, one that does its accounts differently. To be, as Trinh Minh-ha says, a writing woman rather than a written woman—to write my encounters with this difficult and compelling place, rather than to be written by the available storylines. To write in a way that lets many voices in, making a space for a multiplicity that resists reduction. The conventional borders between scholarly and popular writing, between the words of academics and activists, are in need of disruption. There is always a gap between what and how one writes, between what is told and the telling of it. This form of writing offers avenues for reflection on these asymmetries, perhaps more space for the articulations ordinarily excluded.

Carol warned me about the problems of drawing conclusions about Israeli identity practices; she said that Israel is in the midst of a major identity crisis. I wish I could have heard more about that. I assume she was referring to the divisions over the occupied territories, the war in Lebanon, the settlements. Perhaps when I perceive the noose of masculinity and militarism being drawn ever tighter, it is a manifestation of that crisis; hegemonic identities insist on themselves most urgently when they are under challenge.

May 14

TONIGHT I WAS one of the last people to leave the open square in front of the dining room where people chat and children play after supper. I was contemplating a piece of paper that had blown toward me on the warm evening breeze, a fuzzy reproduction of a picture of a wanted "terrorist" who had escaped Israeli custody and was at large in the Ashkelon/Beer Sheva area. Yesterday I returned from Beer Sheva on the bus. When I got home Gili told me he and the family had been worried about me, fearing the bus might be a target of a terrorist attack. Today, these mobile alarms have been circulating everywhere, passing from hand to hand in the dining room, the workplaces, the schools. The photo is dark, indistinct, as is the whole idea of "terrorist" in Israel: there is too much disguised turbulence in that category for me to use it. I want to know who the man is, what was his crime: was he planting bombs on Israeli school buses, or defending his home against the bulldozers, or some other act on that slippery continuum between freedom fighter and terrorist? I want to know, if I met him, would I want to help him or turn him in? And I know that none of these questions would matter very much if a stray bullet came my way. Then, my own questions begin to bother me almost as much as the questions my friends and family here do not ask; I wonder, where can I find the resources to resist the moral dualisms of this troubled land, to refrain from simply reproducing the self-serving, other-denying discourse of good guys and bad guys? I stared at the dim picture on the fugitive wanted poster, but it offered me no answers.

May 15

I AM THINKING about Carol's comment concerning Israel's identity crisis. I'm reading Jacobo Timmerman's *The Longest War*, his searing, self-searching analysis of Israel's invasion of Lebanon. As his own son leaves for the front, and eventually serves time in a military prison for refusing to return, Timmerman examines the crises of moral and political life occasioned by this war. In no other war had Israelis understood themselves to be aggressors. Certainly not in 1948, when the Zionist enterprise protected against any infusion of the Arab perspective. It was a War of Independence, not (as Palestinians remember) The Catastrophe of 1948; the Arabs did not flee real or imagined terrors; they simply "left." Not in 1956, the war in the Sinai; not in 1967, when Jerusalem was liberated (not occupied); not in 1973, the nearly disastrous Yom Kippur War (not the Ramadan war). Of course there were always calls for peace, and warnings about the malevolent consequences of occupation for Jewish identity and security. But these reservations were marginal to what passed as a national consensus.

Nineteen eighty two was different; the war in Lebanon drew widespread protest from soldiers as well as citizens. Dissenting soldiers interviewed after the Lebanon War spoke with bitterness about waste, stupidity, immorality, deceit. A marked contrast with the memories of necessity and collective destiny recorded after the Six-Day War. Israel has had its Vietnam.

Israeli soldiers sometimes speak of their army in terms of purity. They call it *tahor neshek,* a purity of arms. The ethic of the noble soldier using the minimal necessary force to defend his community against an implacable enemy clashed painfully with the experience of an aggressive war against a largely civilian population. The friction generated what Bakhtin might call a double-voiced discourse in Israel. A double-voiced discourse accommodates two different kinds of speech at the same time. It contains a potential dialogue of opposing world views, reflecting the diversity and tumult within what seems to be a shared language. Begin and Sharon called on the ethic of the purity of arms to define the war as inevitable, necessary, as part of a quest for peace. With predictable rhetorical excess,

Begin labeled Arafat "another Hitler." (Arafat returned the favor, contributing further to the over-saturated analogy.) Many of Begin's and Sharon's supporters took refuge in the standard Israeli discipline surrounding war: don't criticize the war while it is happening; stand by your men. Of course Israel is not unique in this regard; I am reminded of the nauseating yellow ribbons and "support our boys" rhetoric in the U.S. during the Gulf War. But in a nation with a citizen army this mandate to loyalty via silence is overwhelming.

The ethic of the purity of arms also generated a critique of the Lebanon war, and subsequently of the occupation. This second voice takes the purity of arms not as an excuse but as a standard, a moral imperative. This voice put hundreds of thousands of Israelis into the streets to protest the war, and created the category of conscientious objector for the first time in Israeli military life.

This voice also prevents critics who are grounded in it from assessing the limits of their animating ethos, limits that stem from the hidden dependencies of the two voices upon one another. Both the opponents and the defenders of the Lebanon War share the same identity terrain, where militarism and masculinity intertwine. They differ over how to apply the ethos, how to fulfill the demands of that identity. These are not small differences; they often seem to be tearing Israel apart. But they do not make a space for other, perhaps more fundamental, questions, such as: Is it ever possible for arms to be pure? What self-deceit is likely to ensue from the pretense that a military can be synonymous with virtue? *Tahor neshek* encourages a slide from morally sensitive soldier to morally justified war to morally depraved or inconsequential enemy. If our arms are pure, and they are fighting us, then theirs must be tainted. Since we are reluctant to fight, our wars must be necessary and justified. The identity practices embedded in the ethos of purity of arms produce the kinds of people who are prepared for, resigned to, military solutions, rather than searching for political ones.

May 16

TODAY WAS SHABBAT, the only day of the week with no work or school. It was a hot, lazy day. Narkis, Aviv and I took the kids on a wagon trip, riding behind the tractor through the fields and orchards of the kibbutz. We picked the sweet pink grapefruit and Narkis and I ate them, the juice running down our arms and dripping off our elbows. The kids preferred the oranges; Aviv held them each up in turn (except Ari, of course, who slept through the whole thing) to pick the fruit off the trees. Oren was delighted with the carrot he pulled up out of the ground. We wiped off the dirt and ate the carrots as we rode.

Narkis's love for her kibbutz is straightforward and genuine. For her, it is simply home. She sometimes says, in her halting English, with sweeping gestures around, "I love it here." This can be applied to any number of places and situations: the noisy dining room where families cluster and friends chat; the playgrounds for the children; the fields whose spring green is now turning to summer brown. Her sense of belonging is complete, undisturbed by reservations or by that accursed attention to the incompleteness of things that Nietzsche teaches. It is not that she has no criticisms of her society, but that her objections issue from, without disturbing, her fundamental sense of being at home. The characteristic fuck-ups and slow downs on the kibbutz, which so infuriate Gili and make him urgently seek change, seem to slide off Narkis; she just shrugs, and goes about her business. She thrives here, as do her children. Her unqualified sense of belonging is enviable. She says about "the Arabs," simply, "I don't like them; they don't like me; let them have their own land and stop the fighting." For her, it is a sensible resolution, and needs no long, agonizing discussion. I sometimes fear her reaction to the thoughts that I put on these pages. I do not want to lose her love, and I would not disturb her peace.

Yet her at-homeness also unsettles me—how can a person root herself so thoroughly in a place that is so contested? It requires an active indifference to the raw and bitter struggles haunting Israel, deferred onto the occupied territories and beyond. In his powerful book about the territories, *The Yellow Wind*, David Grossman talks about how he and other Israeli Jews train themselves to look at Arabs with a kind of blurred vision, a selective gaze that avoids both the individuality of each Palestinian and their collective chiding presence.(p. 19) One must work at not seeing.

May 25

TODAY IS *YOM HA BECURIM*, an agricultural holiday celebrating new life and the productivity of the land. After dinner most people made their way over to the large open hillside near Narkis's house to watch the parade. It was a lovely evening, fragrant and softly lit. Wagons filled with the produce from kibbutz fields and orchards wheeled past—carrots, oranges, grapefruit, watermelons. potatoes, beans. One tractor pulled a small trailer containing one of the new calves. Another boasted a small flock of baby chicks. At the end of the parade came the baby people—the newest generation of kibbutz children. Ari rode on the proud shoulders of his grandfather, claiming his place in this celebration of life.

One day when I was taking a short cut from our house to the kibbutz factory, to make use of the computer facilities there, I passed the area where the calves are usually kept. Row after row of small black and white animals were penned into tiny cement prisons, cages so small they could not run, walk, or even turn around. The visual effect was shocking; I felt like I had stumbled into a penal colony. At lunch that day I ran into Dov's old friend Tomer and asked him why the calves had to be tortured that way. Between his limited English and my limited Hebrew, the conversation was not very satisfying, but I gathered this form of incarceration was deemed necessary to prepare the young animals for market. I could not bear the dreary pens and the confined bodies. I found other routes to take to the factory.

After the parade, I presume that the demonstration calf was returned to his confinement. We went to Narkis's house for cake and coffee, and for pleasant conversation punctuated by the laughter of children.

May 28

So much has been happening. The news has been even grimmer than usual. A few days ago an Arab man from Gaza stabbed a 15-year-old girl who was waiting at a bus stop in Bat Yam, near Tel Aviv, where Aviv's parents live. She died. The man is in custody. Crowds of angry Bat Yam residents took to the streets, beating up Arabs; the

Arab workers hid in terror in basements, on roofs, wherever they could find safety. Some Jews in the town tried to protect the Arabs from the hostile crowd; the police and IDF tried to restore order; but for several days there were angry demonstrations and attacks on Arabs. Activists from the Kahane party led chants of "Death to Arabs."

The girl's name was Helena Rapp. Her father's anguish turned to racial violence. (No mention was made in the paper of her mother.) I don't know the name of the Arab in custody. The Police Ministry has closed Gaza Strip "indefinitely" following the murder, thus keeping thousands of Palestinians from going to their jobs in Israel. It is a grisly echo of the riots in Los Angeles last month, except here people don't loot and burn property. But the same racial hatred festers.

After the killing some Arabs from Gaza came across the border and burnt some fields in two kibbutzim near here. We are three kilometers from Gaza. Last night Arabs from Gaza stole three bulls from the kibbutz; they were later recovered. My personal sense of unquiet grows. The most recent killings (Helena Rapp is one of several recent stabbings) are not by organized groups; no one claims responsibility for them. They seem to be committed by individual Arab men who decide to kill Jews following some personal grievance; Helena Rapp's killer, according to the *Jerusalem Post*, was angry because a Jewish contractor did not hire him. The violence is arbitrary and frequent.

I am having difficulty writing about this. I have tried several times to write "Palestinian" instead of "Arab," to counter the ubiquitous drone of "the Arabs" in everyday discourse. But something in me resists. Partly it is that everyone else says "Arab," including the newspapers, the television news, and the state, so it is easy to fall into the common parlance. But there is more—I feel personally at risk now. I fear for myself, for Gili and the boys, whenever any of us leave the kibbutz. I live a few kilometers from a lot of people who would kill us if they could. That feeling of insecurity tightens the noose of the hegemonic understandings of self and other. In light of that anxiety, stories about Arabs who protect Jews from assault, as a vegetable seller recently did in Gaza, pass unheeded; instead of unraveling that category of "Arab" by marking some as safe rather than dangerous, it becomes merely a curiosity, a human interest story, the exception that proves the rule. I am being propelled into the dominant discourse not just because it is widely available but because it is grounded in love and fear. It is happening to me.

Let me try to write about something a little less searing. Just before these events took place I went to a fascinating conference on "20 Years of Feminism in Israel" at Givat Haviva, between Tel Aviv and Haifa. Givat Haviva is a wonderful place, a conference center where Jewish and Arab groups work together. It is quiet and lovely there, with pleasant sleeping accommodations and convenient meeting rooms. About 200-300 women came to the conference, and it is the first time I have felt surrounded by like-minded people since I have been in Israel. I am not, after all, the only woman in Israel who doesn't shave her legs! The atmosphere was very pleasant and friendly, and very supportive of children. A wonderful young woman with three kids of her own supervised the child care. I had a fascinating roommate, a 75 year old woman from the U.S. who teaches teachers how to teach dance to children. Anne and I got on very well, and enjoyed comparing notes about the conference. Ari was a big hit; lots of women requested time cuddling with him. There was live music and dancing late into the night. I heard a (perhaps apocryphal) story about a Jewish Orthodox lesbian rock band. . . called the Orthodykes!

Most of the workshops and panels during the three

days were in Hebrew, but I was able to understand a little bit and to get some of it translated by obliging participants. Most of the women spoke English; in fact, many of them spoke Hebrew with decided North American accents. Many are immigrants from the U.S. Most of the attendees were Jewish, a fair number being Sephardic; there were about a dozen Arab women there. It was fascinating to see the category of "Jew" come apart as Sephardic women spoke of the particulars of their lives and identities and the problematic domination of the Ashkenazim in Israeli political and cultural life. Sephardic women, also referred to as "Oriental" or Mizrahi, typically have less formal education and inferior jobs compared with their Ashkenazi peers. Israeli feminism has been largely a movement among Ashkenazi women, for much the same reasons of class and education that have led to white dominance in U.S. feminism. One woman, a well-known feminist named Esther Elam, has been an active political presence for 20 years and had never before revealed in a public setting that she is Sephardic. She stood on the stage and "introduced the other Esther Elam," the one none of us, even those who had known her in feminist circles for years, had met. She "came out" as Sephardic.

The attention at the conference to differences between Sephardic and Ashkenazi Jews (sometimes called an "ethnic" difference in Israel) made me think about comparable differences on our kibbutz. Most members of our kibbutz, and of kibbutzim generally, are Ashkenazim. The widespread visibility of (male) kibbutzniks in leadership positions in the Israeli government and military is, then, also implicitly an Ashkenazi presence. Similarly, the position of the kibbutzim as cultural showpieces (albeit, under the Likud government, economically besieged showpieces) is also, implicitly, an Ashkenazi cultural presence. Sephardim are more likely to be found in the poorer urban areas and the dismal development towns. They occupy an uneasy "in-between" status: lower than the Jews of European descent, but higher than the Palestinians or Israeli Arabs. Gili's family is an exception. Dov and Batsheva are Sephardic, their roots in South America and the Mediterranean. But it doesn't seem to make much difference within our kibbutz. Dov's and Batsheva's status as members of the founding generation, plus their shared secularism, Labor party affiliation, and dedication to the kibbutz, seem to totally outweigh "ethnic" differences.

Some of the debates and arguments at the conference sounded about 10 years old to me. I remarked on that to several women, and was always told that Israeli feminism is about a decade "behind" U.S. feminism. For example, arguments between lesbian and straight women echoed debates from within NOW and other US feminist groups in the late 70s; the straight women were, they claimed, quite ready to accept lesbians but why did the lesbians insist on being so vocal about their sexuality? After all, they [the heterosexual women] don't go around announcing that they are heterosexual to the world...and so on. Of course heterosexual women do "announce" their (approved) sexuality all the time, by the clothes they wear, the company they keep, the secrecy they do not require in their lives, and not least by the defensive response they have toward the lesbian women. I thought the lesbians at the conference were remarkably restrained in responding to all this—those obstinate straight women would have been eaten alive in a U.S. feminist context—but that too may be 10 more years in coming. In another conversation, a woman rather arrogantly claimed that it is up to Arab and Sephardic women to make their claims to her, that she is Ashkenazi and middle class and white and that's her world and if they want her to know about their worlds then they need to get busy and tell her. Uh-oh, I thought, this one's in for some trouble in another few years; the women from the dark-skinned groups are going to tire of her easy assumptions about her preferred status in the world. Maybe her listening skills will improve in the process; I laughed when I found out that she is a therapist!

One of the workshops was on incest. The dismal patterns and practices are similar to what I know from the U.S., with a couple of deadly local twists. The speaker, a therapist who works with incest victims, said that the social pressure to hold "the Jewish family" together is so great that most counselors and social workers do not report incest, even though there is a law requiring them to do so. "The Jewish family" is a nearly sacred category, she claimed. It is in part the fear of "Arab" population growth that elevates Jewish reproduction and dictates the sanctity of the Jewish family. Whenever a society worships "the family," women and children pay. I cringed at her description of case after case of children put back into abusive families so that "the Jewish family" would remain intact. An earlier workshop on incest among Arab families was equally disturbing. The speakers there, some of them Arab women, claimed that incest is a completely taboo topic in Arab families; if a girl becomes pregnant after being molested by a male family member, she is killed. No one must know. It is hard to know how to hear this information: in a primarily Jewish setting one suspects that some kind of Orientalism is taking place (i.e., "look at the Arabs, they're even worse than we are"); yet it is equally difficult to discount the information or to minimize the suffering of the young women who face it.

A high point of the conference was the vigil of Women in Black on Friday afternoon. The evening before there was a panel on feminism and protest politics, and some Women in Black activists were there. One woman spoke about trying to bring women from her kibbutz to the demonstrations. Several women commented on the setback that the Gulf War had posed to the group; they quit meeting during the war, but resumed soon after. One woman spoke angrily about "Arabs" dancing on their rooftops as missiles fell on Tel Aviv. When Palestinians sided with Saddam Hussein, it became even more taboo to be "soft on Arabs." It took a lot of courage to begin the vigils again, and they lost a lot of women. But they have never given up; every Friday from 1:00-2:00, at intersections across the country, women dressed in black stand in silence holding signs that say "Stop the Occupation" and "Talk about Peace." They began in January of 1988, soon after the outbreak of the Intifada. Many different women come out for the vigils; they have many different reasons. They are united in their belief that peace must take priority now and that peace requires ending the occupation. Other groups have come out in counter-protest—at our vigil a lone man waving an Israeli flag stood on the other side of the street—but the other groups always give up after some weeks or months, while Women in Black persevere.

The widespread assumption I encountered at the conference that Israeli feminism is a decade or so "behind" U.S. feminism may underestimate the singularity and potency of groups such as Women in Black. Why should there be a single trajectory for feminism to take? U.S. and Israeli women do not inhabit identical histories or cultures; the living ensemble of their social relations do not fully correspond. Because many of the women at the conference are immigrants from the U.S., they may have U.S. models too firmly fixed in their minds. But since they are frequently dismissed by *sabra* (native born) women and men as an illegitimate "import" rather than a native grown movement, it is difficult for them to examine these issues without calling themselves entirely into question. Women in Black has been taken as a model for women's peace politics all over the world (including the U.S.), so it is not at all clear who is "ahead" and who is "behind."

Ours was a very big vigil, probably 75 women, as we from the conference swelled the ranks of the local activists. It was a festive, celebratory occasion; Arab and Jewish women (and at least one infidel) standing together, making common cause for peace. Unlike some of the vigils I had read about, in which the demonstrators are spit upon or pelted with eggs and tomatoes, ours got a fairly positive response; I'd say that over half of the drivers responded with some words or gestures of agreement and encouragement. There was also, of course, the usual barrage of "fuck yous" and the usual sexual accusations. "Whores of Arafat" seems to be a favorite. I was told that the area around Givat Haviva has a large Arab population, which partly explains the positive response. I talked to some women about the atmosphere of vigils in other places, and got a mixed response. One woman said that the one time she stood in the vigil in Jerusalem, they were gassed by the police; another woman who frequently stands in Jerusalem said that the mood varies, sometimes serious and surrounded by hostility, other times more festive. Nabila Espanioly, an Israeli Arab feminist who attended the conference, writes in "Palestinian Women in Israel Respond to the *Intifada*" about the different response to Women in Black in Nazareth. In that largely Arab city the women's silent protest was met with "God bless you" and "God give you the strength to carry on." (p. 147) Espanioly also comments on the relative isolation of Women in Black; while the different groups are connected by their newsletter and occasional conferences, their activities are rarely reported in the mainstream media.

I was pleased to interview Gila Svirsky, a Woman in Black activist, at the conference. A very high-energy woman, she relaxed for a few minutes to cuddle Ari and speak with me about politics. Gila's optimism about the upcoming elections, and the desire for peace in the country, cheered me. I have observed a widespread fatalism about war in Israel; she sees a more widespread desire to take action to end it now. Rabin, leader of the Labor party, is arguing that the time is right: the USSR no longer can support Syria and Iraq; the U.S. is pushing for a settlement; the Israeli economy desperately needs to invest in jobs and education, not in the military; the settlements in the territories do not enhance Israeli security and should be stopped. These are all cogent arguments; but cogent arguments don't seem to go very far with people whose blood stirs at the sight of waving flags and the chant of "death to Arabs." Gila recognized her opponents, but insisted that the majority of Israeli Jews would support some territorial compromise to achieve peace. As she and Ari played together she reflected on the costs of the occupation for Israel:

"I want to end the occupation because of what it does to Israel. It corrupts Israeli society, corrupts our Judaism, makes a travesty of our Zionism, distorts what this country was supposed to be about. It turns us into oppressors of other people. . . we who have suffered oppression for so long should have learned the lesson of how not to become oppressors. It distorts and reshuffles our priorities from basic decent values—family life, education, mutual respect—into values of militarism and subjugation. . . . It cuts into the amount of money we can spend on education, on social services, on welfare, on creating jobs, on absorbing Russian and Ethiopian immigrants. It cuts into everything that we're able to do with our national resources."

Emphatically, with irony, she reflected, "I don't want to spend my time worrying about terrorism."

From discussions with women at the conference, as well as from my reading, I've become a bit clearer on the complexities of the Intifada. It was/is an agglomeration of activities, events, and practices: a nonviolent tax revolt; the organization of local committees to provide education and services, usually by women; various kinds of passive resistance; angry confrontations and stone-throwing; campaigns of solidarity with political prisoners (again, usually by women). The media images of armed resistance are matched by criticism from within the ranks of Palestinian activists of the posturing young men brandishing automatic weapons for the television cameras. In the last week there have been demonstrations in Gaza against the killing of Palestinians thought to be cooperating with Israeli authorities; there is a current split between Hamas and the PLO over Chamber of Commerce elections.

One day when Dov saw Oren throwing pebbles he laughed and said, scornfully, "Intifada." Seeing only one dimension to the Intifada is the same kind of blindness, of self-protection leading to self-destruction, as seeing only one kind of "Arab."

It is often claimed that Palestinian women are liberated by the Intifada; they have taken important roles in sustaining their neighborhoods and families. But what about the counter pull, the negative effects of the normalization of violence and the assertions of nationalism for Palestinian women? During the Gulf War, Israeli feminists believe, violence against women increased dramatically in Israel. There were many more women killed during that year than in previous years. A report from the Academic Study Group in Israel and the Middle East claims that, before the war, there were on average 3-4 wife-murders per year; in the six months following the war, there were 30-40 cases. (p. 9) The feminists I spoke with acknowledged how difficult it is to establish a causal relation here, but are convinced that the heightened atmosphere of violence, combined with the fact that men were sealed in their houses with women, led to increased violence. Galia Golan, a Peace Now activist who is a political scientist at Hebrew University, argues that the curfews imposed on the occupied territories have had a similar effect, confining men in their homes with their families and increasing the violence toward women. Of course one could say that the Intifada is a liberation movement, nothing like the situation in Israel during the Gulf War; but I wonder if nationalism and frustrated masculinity are so different in each case.

May 26

Today I attended a seminar on gender and genre at Beer Sheva University. I really like some of the women there, and I crave the lively feminist presence. I missed Ari today; no little body to cuddle, no endearing smile, no hungry mouth to relieve the pressure building in my breasts. More than that, I sustain a nagging worry when I am away from the kibbutz that something will happen to me, that I will leave my children without a mother.

Niza Yanai commented on why the Intifada and Occupation, and their effect on women in Israel, goes underthematized in feminism and in society generally. She believes that Women in Black are an exception, that despite a visible peace movement, there is avoidance of the issue. The obvious reason is the one I have so personally encountered: feminists too live in this society and have security concerns. Fear of Palestinian violence (I cannot yet use the word terrorism the way they do) makes anything "pro-Arab" suspect. But Niza's point is that women in Israel feel guilty about criticizing anything to do with the army and war, because, while they go to the army, they don't risk life (for the most part), while the men do. They are part of the military, yet protected within it; it is a peculiar status, leaving them little legitimate ground for critique. The young women can perform their obligatory national service without disturbing either the manliness of the military or the conventional femininity of the civilian roles they are expected to resume.

This protected status for women in the military may account for the relative lack of discussion by mothers about their daughters' military obligations. Religious girls are exempt from military service, as are religious boys if they are attending *yeshiva* (Hebrew school). Married women and mothers of children are also exempt. Other young Jewish women serve two years, usually in clerical, medical, or other support functions. Unlike the men, who may be called up for reserve duty as much as three months each year until the age of 55, most women's reserve obligations end at age 24 or at the birth of their first child. I know there are discussions within the military about women's role, with reformers pushing for more active participation of women in combat and others protecting that male preserve. But I hear very little from mothers of young women entering the military. Gili says that the military functions as a giant national dating service; it is the center of youth culture for Israeli Jews. Given the enormous emphasis on marriage and childbirth (a young woman who has not married by age 25 is viewed as an "old maid," and women without children are widely pitied) mothers of daughters may value the marriage opportunities the military makes available.

It was fun to be in a university setting again, to hear the familiar arguments and to once again be in a group in which feminism offers a legitimate context for public discussion. Yael Feldman gave an interesting paper, and observed that "the notorious first person plural of Israeli society" projects a uniformity that suppresses feminist endeavors. I thought of the "cycle of life" skit at the *ulpan*, in which "our" life cycle is Jewish and male; I also thought of the fatalistic shrugs that accompany the familiar refrain "It is our life." Prodding against the seamlessness of that "we," without turning one's back on it altogether, is a tricky business.

After the panel I was included in a luncheon with the participants and others from the university. In a move that probably marked me as both U.S. American and *goya*, I stuck out my hand to shake hands with my new acquaintances. The man sitting across from me smiled politely but refused my hand. Everyone else acted like nothing untoward was happening, so I withdrew the offending female member, belatedly recalling the Orthodox Jewish prohibition on a man touching a woman other than his wife.

May 27

GILI HAD A disturbing conversation with one of the kibbutzniks, a guy from Chile, about his reserve duty. This fellow spoke about arresting Palestinians: his unit would surround the house, break in, herd all the women into one room, search for the suspect, and take him. Often they would have to tear him away from the children clinging to him. They would put all the women in one place because they "made so much noise." He talked about how distressing it was to see the terror of the children and to be the cause of it. He tried to get in the group that secured the perimeter rather than the group that stormed the house so that he wouldn't have to look at the terrified, accusing eyes of the children.

June 1

THIS WEEK HOSTS yet another heavily freighted holiday: Jerusalem Day, marking 25 years since the "reunification" of the city. From the Palestinian point of view, of course, there is little to celebrate; instead, there has been 25 years of occupation. But that view is given little space. The mayor of East Jerusalem pointed out in a *Jerusalem Post* article that the Arabs in East Jerusalem pay equivalent taxes to the Jews in the West, but have fewer services provided. This modest protest was subsumed in an enthusiastic endorsement of Jewish military victory and cultural hegemony.

Today at the *ulpan* we had a lecture about the Battle of Jerusalem by a soldier who fought there 25 years ago. An unassuming personable man in his mid-40s spoke about the battle, showing us the shifting borders on the map and describing the battle strategies. Israelis savor the memory of their wars - this man described the sounds of the different weapons, the intimate proximities of the armies, the view from Jerusalem's hills. His account of the street fighting conveyed the soldiers' fears, the actions of the medics. It is a kind of heroism of the ordinary; Israelis democratize their militarism, offering the image of soldier/hero to every man in uniform, which means nearly every man. The papers are also full of stories of everyman's heroism in the reunification battles. I thought about Nicaragua when I was there, only six years after the revolution. There was little worship of soldiers and battles there; their excitement was about their literacy campaign, their health programs, their poetry workshops. Their predominant self-understanding was anchored in revolutionary hopes; here it is planted firmly in an identity of martyrs and survivors, heroes and victims.

During class we had to write a story to go with a

picture of a young white man, smiling, holding a dark-skinned infant in front of a very dilapidated set of shacks. We all dutifully made up stories about generous white men coming from the West to help needy black children in Africa. Our limited, highly conventionalized vocabularies confined us to this story. We haven't learned the words to tell any other story. I don't know how to talk about indigenous people driven from their land by multinational corporations and greedy local elites. I suppose that would be the case with most introductory language courses. When I first studied Spanish and French, I don't remember learning the vocabulary of political critique. On the other hand, I also don't remember learning the words for "soldier," "border," "war," or "battle," which were early acquisitions in the language arsenals of the *olim hadashim* in our *ulpan*.

June 8

WE'VE JUST HAD a nice adventure in Jerusalem. The four of us stayed for two nights and three days at the YMCA, a beautiful building with a noble tower, dozens of arches, murals, rich wood paneling; not the antiseptic place I always think of as a YMCA. (Then again, most YMCAs don't boast carefully preserved bullet holes in their walls, either.)

I met with several women involved in peace issues here, and I participated in another demonstration of Women in Black. Tamar Rapoport and Sarit Helman from Hebrew University are active in Women in Black, and also are conducting research on the movement. They met us for drinks out on the lovely lanai of the YMCA; we sat for a long time, admiring the view of the King David Hotel across the street, enjoying the carefully manicured grounds of the two hotels, talking intensely about politics, war, children, life. Tamar has carrot-red hair and an ironic presence in her eyes; Sarit is more solemn, slender and direct. These women fill an enormous intellectual gulf for me, one I didn't even fully apprehend until conversations with them highlighted the previous absence. The kibbutz is a compelling place, full of warm and friendly people, great for children. But there are no like-minded people there for me.

I also spoke with Galia Golan, whom I had met before at Givat Haviva. A thoughtful woman with an air of dignity about her, she teaches political science at Hebrew University and is active in Peace Now. She thought out loud with me about why it is difficult to articulate militarism as an issue in Israel: because the indisputable need for some kind of security provides a bloated cover for the military's definition of the term; because it is shocking to many Israeli Jews to think of their country as militaristic, and they respond defensively; because the army is not "out there," but is made up of one's parents, children, and friends. "I have very warm and respectful feelings about the army," she remarked. Israeli pride in the army has been somewhat tarnished by the invasion of Lebanon and the Intifada; she believes it has lost a bit of its aura. But it is still central to Israeli Jewish identity, so much so that any small blemish on its mystique is significant. "It's us."

This was a big Women in Black vigil, several hundred people, marking the 25th anniversary of the occupation. There were lots of angry counter-demonstrators, mostly adolescent boys from the religious nationalist movements. I found a pile of signs and studied them for a moment, choosing between "Stop the Occupation" and "Talk to the PLO." I saw several women I had met at the conference at Givat Haviva—Israel is indeed a small place, and feminism within Israel a much smaller place still. Passers-by were alternately hostile, withdrawn, occasionally supportive...but the reception was much colder in Jerusalem than in Givat Haviva.

After the vigil I went with Tamar and Sarit to a peace march in an Arab neighborhood in East Jerusalem. It is no exaggeration to say that there were as many police as demonstrators. Tamar spoke in a friendly, joking way to several of the police, whom she seemed to recognize. After the solidarity and conviction of the Women in Black vigil, the march was poorly organized, undirected, lacking in spirit. We milled around for awhile, marched a short distance through the village, got very hungry and thirsty, received a fairly indifferent response (except from the sidewalk food vendors—they were glad to see us), and left.

That night Gili and I took the kids for a walk through Jerusalem, in the neighborhoods just outside the Old City. It is a beautiful city, especially at night, with all the lights, the little winding streets, lovely old buildings, pleasant parks. The granite wall around the Old City glows and beckons. It seems a peaceful city, dignified and serene.

June 9

SEVERAL TIMES DURING my interviews and conversations I have heard someone say, about some other group perceived as a bit farther to the left, they've "gone too far." Dov says that the organizers of the Givat Haviva conference have "gone too far." Galia Golan says that Women in Black have "gone too far." Tamar and Sarit say that *Challenge* magazine, an English-language publication of the Israeli Left, has "gone too far." What does this mean? Sarit and Tamar interpreted it to mean that the offenders have, from the speaker's point of view, become too sympathetic to the Palestinians, to the point of identifying completely with them and forgetting that there is a legitimate Jewish point of view. But what is it, exactly, that is endangered? Is this a sexual anxiety, a fear of intimacy with the Other? Perhaps the offender has gone too far the way teenagers in the back seat of a Plymouth might go too far, committing an irrevocable act, somehow destroying their innocence and purity. Is this why the epithet "whores of Arafat" is so frequently flung at Women in Black? Or is it more generally about acceptance, a fear of accepting the other so they're not so Other any more, and you, then, are not so special, so unique, so separate? Maybe "whores of Arafat" is similar to the white epithet "nigger-lover," designating not primarily a sexual connection but a general, and illegitimate, acceptance of the other. And since acceptance of the other might be the first step toward the forbidden intimacy, the two could be wound up together. I wonder what "going too far" means from the Palestinian point of view.

The phrase "going too far" connects identity with a spatial metaphor, and suggests a link with the territorial dimensions of identity practices in Israel, and in all modern nation states. Each people has/demands its proper place, always defined as a state. Jonathan Boyarin points out that the creation of the state of Israel was a convenient solution to Europe's "Jewish problem"; it got rid of the Jews without having to examine the state policies in Europe and North America that helped create the crises of Jewry.(p. 121) Presumably the state of Israel will someday figure out that the creation of a Palestinian state could perform a similar clearing operation. Meanwhile, the territorialization of identity gives it a sharp either/or component: either our land or their land. Palestinians and Israelis both struggle to delineate their collective identities by establishing/maintaining themselves as nation states. Identity collapses into (existing or sought for) state power.

Boyarin gives a particularly striking example of the conflation of identity and territory: he cites "the recent arrest of an Israeli Jewish educator named Arna Mer on charges of 'identifying with the enemy.' The specific act she was censured for was going to the Palestinian town of Jenin to provide educational materials to school children." (p. 123) Collective identity based on control of territory sponsors a zero-sum calculation: either we belong here or they do. Not both. No sharing.

One can imagine collective identities that are deterritorialized, knit together in some other ways, perhaps from shared memories, daily practices, concrete needs, specific relationships to people, locations, and histories. Such productions would be more narrative than territorial; they might not be so exclusive because they are not so relentlessly spatial. Connection to a particular place could still be honored as one dimension of identity, but its intensities could be leavened by less competitive claims. Participation in such identities could be self-consciously partial, constructed, mobile; something one does and re-does everyday, not a docile space one simply occupies and controls. Empathy across collective identities constructed as fluid and open could enrich, rather than endanger, one's sense of who one is.

Deterritorializing identity is a cultural shift that would probably sound a bit premature to Palestinian ears; after all, I have a state, with the securities (and liabilities) of citizenship, from which to dream about uncoupling identity. So do the Jews. The Palestinians do not. Certainly everyone needs a secure and autonomous place to live; but must identity be so intensely bound up with the exclusive governance of territory? All territorializations of identity have a strong "lets pretend" dimension—in denying that anyone was there before, in ignoring competing claims, in cultivating a myopic nostalgia for lost origins. It may be that a deterritorializing of identity is a more promising path toward securing a Palestinian homeland than is the current battle between mutually exclusive claims to belong.

In that sort of world, Arna Mer's act would not need to be one either of a traitor or a hero. It could simply be a life.

June 10

GILA SVIRSKY HAS an essay on "Women in Black" in *Jewish Women's Call for Peace.* With Women in Black, she has come to believe that "women have characteristic feelings about peace," that "women have a special sensitivity that they bring to situations of hostility—motherliness, nurturing, aversion to suffering." (p. 8) She recognizes that there are women who don't manifest these attitudes and behaviors, explicitly racist women among the religious nationalist party supporters, but she sees them as "aberrations." (p. 8) I cringe at this naturalization of feminist peace politics. Gila does to the category "women" what the hegemonic self-understandings in Israeli life do to the categories "Jew" and "Arab"—put them beyond analysis, beyond history, in some natural realm where their alleged traits can be construed as fundamental, requiring no explanation. But Gila develops some interesting reflections about a double connection between women and peace:

> When I go to demonstrations about Israel's occupation of the West Bank and Gaza Strip, against violence (on both sides), in favor of negotiation—they are there in great numbers: women from the rape crisis centers

> around Israel, from the battered women's shelters, from the health hotlines, from the antipornography groups. Those who are sensitive to the issue of violence against women apply that lesson to all forms of violence and oppression. The feminist movement in Israel appears solidly (though unofficially) in the peace camp. (p. 8)

She goes on to characterize their reception at vigils:

> But because we are women, we are also subject to a double load of abuse when we stand up and protest the uses of war and violence. Women's peace activities, more than any other, seem to invite intense verbal abuse, mostly sexual in nature." (p. 8)

Mixed-sex demonstrations elicit more politically oriented abuse—accusations that the demonstrators are "traitors," "anti-Semitic Jews," that they "forgot the Holocaust." (p. 8) The specifically sexual verbal epithets are mostly reserved for the all-women vigils.

Why? If the connection of women to peace is culturally widespread, written into women's traditional practices as mothers, wives, caretakers, then wouldn't even opponents of feminism come to expect it, to dismiss it as "just the way women are"? Perhaps that acceptance is withheld because, while women are expected to oppose violence, we are also expected to stay out of public life, so our opposition is never supposed to be politically expressed. Private griefs, like Calanit's and Geula's, are legitimate; not public ones, like Gila's. And because women are defined in basically private, domestic, sexual terms, our transgressions into public life elicit responses in those terms: e.g., "whores of the Arabs," "what you need as a good fuck," and so forth. (The "other side" returns the favor: Palestinian children throwing stones at Israeli soldiers frequently taunt them by shouting "Your sister fucks an Arab!") So the same ideology that connects women with peace (via mothering and caretaking) also delegitimates our pursuit of peace (stay out of politics, leave it to the men) and provides the ideological ammunition to attack us when we do speak publicly (threats of sexual violence).

What a tricky, potent, and unreliable ideology, this business of mothering/caretaking/women's experiences in homes and families. Mothering filtered through the screens of patriarchy is an uncertain basis for politics. The resistances attendant to a politicized mothering are powerful, but are thoroughly insinuated into the grounds for their repression and dismissal.

June 15

TODAY WHEN I came home from the *ulpan* we drove into the kibbutz and there were police everywhere, a roadblock at the gate—it seems that someone had parked a car near the kibbutz gates and left it there, and of course the guards suspected a bomb. Our bus sat outside the gate for some time while the officials checked the car and looked for the owner. I tried to figure out what was going on by listening to the conversations around me, but finally I asked in English, my voice striving to sound calm. My sons were inside and I could not get to them. I don't know the outcome of it all, but we were eventually allowed in, and evidently there was no bomb.

June 18

OUR MORNING RITUAL has become quite pleasant and familiar. Since breakfast, lunch and snacks are provided for the kids at the *beit tinnock* and the *gan*, there is a lot less work to do in the mornings. We stick Ari in the baby carriage provided by the kibbutz and Gili walks him to the *beit tinnock* while Oren and I stroll to the *gan*, checking out different plants and animals that we pass on the way. Gili and I rendezvous at the dining room, where I grab some breakfast (I will never get used to cold, hard toast!) and run out to catch the bus to the *ulpan* I often sit with a young man named Galil, who is a student at the college where our *ulpan* meets. He obligingly helps me with my homework, and we often discuss the coming elections.

Galil is a Meretz supporter. Meretz is a coalition party made up of the Citizen's Party (a peace party with some feminist leanings), the socialists, and the capitalists! Only in Israel, I think to myself. The three parties are united on their pursuit of peace with the Palestinians. Gili went to a Meretz meeting on the kibbutz recently, and only about a dozen people showed up; Labor is by far the more popular party here.

Galil is a tall, earnest young man with reddish hair and a thoughtful expression. His desire for peace, for an end to the occupation, speaks a powerful counterbalance to the fatalism and resignation I more often hear. This election is "Israel's last chance," Galil tells me. If the left does not win this time, he is going to leave the country.

The decision to leave Israel is a heavily freighted one. When a Jew immigrates to Israel, it is called making *aliyah*. Far more than a geographical relocation, *aliyah* is a moral ascent, a going up. *Yerida* is the opposite; not just emigration, it is a going down, a descent; it is widely interpreted as a rejection of Israeli life and culture. The terms of entrance and exit, like other political calculations here, reflect a morally dualistic understanding. There is little room here for someone like my husband to articulate his comings and goings; Gili left Israel not because he rejected his country, but because he wanted to see the world. He settled in Hawaii because he loved Hawaii, not because he hated Israel. Nor is there much space to articulate my family's periodic returns—this is our third visit in five years, the first occurring when Oren was newborn. In my *ulpan* there are only two categories of students: new immigrants and tourists. I am therefore called a "tourist" because my sojourn in Israel is temporary rather than permanent; there is, seemingly, no other category of relationship to Israel. But our kibbutz shows a willingness to allow us a different status—to acknowledge that, while we don't intend to stay, we plan frequently to return. Our circular pattern of coming and going is neither *aliyah* nor *yerida*, but a periodic moving through an identity position that history and desire have made available to us.

Galil contemplates *yerida* within the more conventional moral dualism, only he reverses it; he does not want to live in a society that is capable of such a war. He reminds me a great deal of my generation of U.S. college students during the Vietnam war, reflecting that same moral heart sickness, the disappointment that one's native land could so let one down. I asked Galil where he would go, what he would do. "I don't know," he replied, gazing at me with thoughtful eyes. He paused, and smiled. "The world is big."

June 23

TODAY IS ELECTION day. A lot of people here are hopeful that Labor will win, that is, get a big enough minority vote to put together a governing coalition. It has been 12 years since Labor was voted out and the Likud came to power, 12 years since the tiny ultranationalist, ultrareligious parties rose to power in the coalition system—and 12 years since Gili last voted in an Israeli election. He's hoping to effect another turnaround. Gili and I support Meretz, the same leftist party that Galil endorses. An acquaintance of mine from Political Science conferences and from Women in Black, Naomi Chazan, is a candidate. Our hope is that Labor will get the most votes, will make a coalition with Meretz, and Meretz will have some influence on Labor policies. If Likud wins, it will be more of the same. Ironically, Likud won last time on the promise that only the Likud can make peace (sort of like "Only Nixon can go to China"). But their track record for the last four years makes that claim laughable. They are not willing to negotiate with the Palestinians in any serious way.

June 24

I AM SO relieved. . . it feels like a miracle has happened. Meretz got twelve seats (out of 120) and Labor got 45. Together they are only five seats short of an absolute majority. Meretz's showing was really strong; there IS a substantial voice for peace in this country. Finally the Likud is out, and with it hopefully the nastier of the nationalist groups. I'm glad Naomi got in; she will be a strong voice for feminism and peace.

June 25

IT IS PREDICTABLE, but still so upsetting...Labor is trying to distance itself from Meretz, claiming it wants a "broad" government, not one of "the extreme right or the extreme left."

Damn Rabin. He knows he needs Meretz, but he doesn't want to rely on them or be beholden to them. It will take a lot of work on their part to have the say their mandate deserves.

How interesting it is to live in a country where there is some life in national politics, where the desperate issues the society faces have some (albeit limited) presence in electoral debate. I say some. The election campaigns (Israelis are more frank than Americans—they call it propaganda) were appalling. The religious nationalist commercials were simply racist—pictures of masked Palestinians, looming ominously or throwing rocks into windshields or marching facelessly, were featured, then Xed out (as in the "no smoking" signs) i.e., "no Arabs." Rooms of bearded rabbis with colored glasses (why in the world do they wear those colored glasses?) and medieval trappings spoke about "greater Israel." (i.e., IT'S ALL OURS!) Meretz was the only party that spoke with any sense about issues; Labor put down Likud and Likud tried to be heartwarming. But still, there are at least some choices for voters here, and one feels like it matters who one votes for. Gili voted for the first time in twelve years, and again there was a reversal (this time Likud out, Labor in); he says if they need him again, they should let him know.

June 26

RABIN IS STILL dancing around his coalition partners. He wants to distinguish between "security" and "political" settlements, and keep the first while slowing the second. The paper said that the existing permits for building in the territories will keep settlement going for a couple of years out of inertia. Still, I am cautiously optimistic. Now at least the government talks of less rather than more settlement; and they "will not talk to the PLO" but they will talk to Palestinians from the territories who can talk to anyone they choose. There is even talk of changing the law outlawing contact with the PLO.

Yesterday I went into Gaza twice, dropping off and picking up workers for the kibbutz factory. It was appalling. . . the lines into and out of Gaza at rush hour are HOURS long, for the Palestinians; people who have Israeli plates (like our minibus) can weave in and out of the traffic and crowd to the front of the line. (If the factory manager, who was driving, ever needs a job, he would be a great cab driver in New York City.) It must take the Gazans hours every day to get to and from work. I imagine the parents waiting restlessly or anxiously in line in their vehicles, wondering what their children are doing. When we got through the checkpoint, there were heavily armed soldiers everywhere, with looks of arrogance and boredom in their eyes; the ubiquitous barbed wire, the desolation, the small children selling good or trinkets, lots of people trying to catch rides. Many people seemed simply to be waiting. We let our passengers off ("our Arabs"—a Gazan family with a long history of ties to our kibbutz) and left.

July 10

TODAY'S *JERUSALEM POST* carried a fascinating article on the current "national craze" of courses preparing high school boys for the army and improving their chances of being selected for an "elite unit." Those electing not to take the course can instead purchase the video, a "'Jane Fonda Workout' for future soldiers," promoted as "ideal viewing for the entire family." Course creator Yuval Eliam, "army preparation guru," stresses that he is "an educational figure, not some kind of macho man." He is striving to create a "prepared generation," "ready and informed about what's going to happen." There is, of course, no companion article detailing any national craze for, say, conflict resolution courses, no large scale efforts to prepare a generation for the hard work of peace.

Women soldiers are present in this happy account of budding young soldiers only indirectly and through denial. While Israeli girls also face compulsory military service, these prep courses are, it seems, only for boys. "Eliam even brings in the students' girlfriends, so that both sides know what to expect from the relationship once one of them enters the army." There is a remarkable slippage in this sentence: it recognizes that the "girlfriends" too will enter the army, yet reserves the position of student-preparing-for-the-army for males. The obligatory academic observer is brought in to comment on these proceedings: Hannah Herzog, lecturer on Israeli society at Tel Aviv University, points out that the high price of these preparation courses works against the poor and undermines the opportunities for upward mobility traditionally made available to the disadvantaged through the military. No one thinks to regret the lack of upward mobility via military service for women, or for the Israeli Arabs who are barred from military service altogether. Nor does anyone comment on the lesser forms of citizenship implicitly bestowed upon Jewish women and Israeli Arabs in a society in which to be a citizen is to be a fighter is to be a man.

July 18

We made a last trip to Beer Shiva today, all four of us, to do a bit of shopping at the large outdoor market, to see the Bedouin market where sheep and camels are traded, to visit some friends at the university one last time. Gili and I took the kids to play in the bright sunshine of an open, grassy courtyard on campus. A young man sat quietly under a tree in one corner of the yard, reading a book, his machine gun across his knees. His student job is to guard the university from attack. He answered my questions patiently, pausing in his reading yet eager to get back to his book. No, he is not in the military; he has finished his military duty and now attends the university. Yes, I can take his picture; he smiles from the shadows, his book propped against the barrel of the gun. Yes, he likes his job; it gives him a lot of time to study. May it always be so.

July 23

THIS IS OUR last week in the kibbutz. On Sunday we fly to Indiana to be with my family for a few days, then on to Hawai`i on August 1. We had a small going-away party at my class at the *ulpan*; they sang some farewell songs, the typical sentimental but also compelling ballads that we have been learning during the class. Raisa brought a remarkable cake; I made brownies, popcorn (which the Russians loved), pretzels and dip; I tried to make very "American" stuff. I took Hawaiian music and photo books to show the others, and flowers as a gift for Smadar. Smadar and Ronit (the head of the school, Dov's friend and cousin by marriage) made little speeches about me, a very Israeli thing to do on such an occasion: they talked about my desire to learn Hebrew so that my sons can learn it too. The class gave me a going-away gift of a photo album and a flowery card with inscriptions from each person in the class. I want to record their names, so I won't forget: Alex and Raisa, from a part of the Ukraine near Chernobyl, I think the name is something like Chernatzka; their son Max, and his wife Roxanne, who was an even worse student of Hebrew than I was; sweet Karen, from England; young Tamara, from Los Angeles; Rosa and Rudolpho, my friends from Columbia and Chile; Marianne from Argentina; Anatole, with a three year old daughter; Luda, the baker; Anna, the musician; Tayia and Grecia, with young Uri who always wanted to go to the pool; Sima, whose baby was always sick; Gady and Lola, who gave me the wooden pen as a going away gift. The last ones all from Russia. I was very moved by their friendship and respect. I wonder what will happen to these *olim hadashim.* Many of the kibbutzniks resent the Russian immigrants, who have a reputation for racism toward the Ethiopian Jews and for viewing Israel in terms of economic opportunity rather than Zionist commitment. Often debates rage in our classroom, political and economic discussions in a furious mix of Hebrew, English, Spanish, and Russian; it is hard to follow the specifics, but the tone is always urgent, sometimes desperate. They have put so much on the line to come here, left behind lives and families; "home" has become truly problematic for them, and their struggle with that ambivalence is often painful to watch.

I wish I could stay another month and finish the class. I was not a great student, but I studied hard. Sometimes I surprise myself with my ability to speak and understand; other times I am totally at a loss. But next time we come to Israel I will at least have this base to work from, and each time I will learn more.

My class went to Jerusalem this week. I didn't go with them, because Gili and I went on our own to visit friends. But I know from what Jana told me about her class trip that it was another formative experience in the creation of new Israelis: first stop is the terrible, draining Holocaust museum, A Hand and a Name (*Yad V'Shem*), where the children's exhibit, the hall of names of all known victims, the last, tiny shoe of some lost, murdered baby, wring all hope from your heart. Then to the museum of military struggle, marking the battle for Jerusalem. And the Wailing Wall. And the museums of archeology. The Islamic and Christian claims on Jerusalem's past receive minor, passing mention, a footnote to the history that really counts. The winning history is, of course, the long and tortured history of the Jews, continually, selectively, reinvoked to weave an identity around danger and necessity, abandonment and destruction, fierce claims of entitlement, homelessness, and exile. Not a fertile soil for peace; yet like a weed, peace can grow in unexpected places.

Instead of going with my class, Gili and the kids and I went to visit as old friend of Gili's from the kibbutz. Aria and Josephine and baby Laurie (the older kids are in France visiting grandparents) welcomed us with the warmest hospitality. They made us splendid meals, introduced us to their friends, took us to the synagogue in a nearby hospital to see the lovely Chagall windows (where one of the beautiful stained glass windows still boasts a bullet hole, left by Chagall himself when he repaired the windows after the Six Day War). Aria is an officer in the border guard. His job is to keep the Palestinians in their place. He points out, probably rightly, that the Israeli occupation forces are very careful to avoid civilian loss of life when possible, to minimize confrontation. For example, the recent crisis at the university on the West Bank (the Israelis claimed that there were armed terrorists trying to influence the student elections, which were a contest, again, between PLO and Hamas; the students denied it) was resolved by compromise, probably because James Baker was coming to push the peace talks, the Rabin government had just gotten in the saddle, nobody wanted a major crisis at that moment. Aria is probably right; as occupations go, this one is not particularly brutal; its tactics go more for humiliation and control than extermination. But it is no less effective in creating enmity and self-righteousness, in fostering militarism, than a more murderous regime would be. Aria is resigned to continued fighting; he sees no effective leadership among the Palestinians with whom to negotiate. Rather than seeing a valuable opportunity to negotiate with the more moderate PLO factions, strengthening their position vis-a-vis Hamas, he sees only another reason to continue the war. Among his peers, his views are probably moderate.

I spent some time with Erella Shadmi, a radical feminist who teaches feminist theory at Beer Sheva. She considers the whole Israeli feminist movement to be far too legalistic, not radical enough. (A lot of women seem to think that, I think there must be more of them than they believe.) She sees certain taboos within Israeli feminism—an avoidance of lesbianism, for example, and women in the military, and women's relation to fundamentalism. The most visible feminists, she argues, talk about less explosive topics, such as discrimination and parity. I am again reminded of debates within U.S. feminism ten to fifteen years ago, when liberal feminism dominated the national feminist agenda while, at the same time, many women frustrated with those limits were pushing against them in local contexts. Erella says that the public discussion and display of lesbianism at the Givat Haviva conference was one of the first such occasions for Israeli feminists. Evidently, what seemed to my U.S. American eyes and ears to be a very mild and mannerly assertion of lesbianism was fairly path breaking here.

Erella used to be a police officer too, and she and Aria talked shop for awhile. She is a striking woman, with lovely, long curly brown hair. Her eight-year-old daughter played with Oren while we talked. Like Aria, she maintained that the Israeli forces are not particularly brutal; and that the Palestinians have suffered more from the other Arab nations than from Israel. Unlike him, she spoke of her militant opposition to the occupation.

"The military," she remarked, "is the most important institution in the country." She spoke of the pride most Israeli Jews have in their military service, and the clear superiority accorded to the role of men there. She talked about the taken-for-grantedness of military participation: "My daughter asked me when she was two years old, 'Mother, do I have to go to the army?'...A mother's main duty is to raise a baby to be a soldier." The words of other Israeli women echoed in my ears: Galia Golan: "It's us"; Geula and Calanit: "It is our life"; Yael Feldman's comment about "the notorious first person plural of Israeli society." That "we/us/ours" not only marginalizes women and excludes Israeli Arabs, it also completely embricates military practices into the prevailing identity formations. I thought of Oren, who sometimes voices a fear of war but never anticipates being a soldier. How would I mother him differently, if I knew that military service would be required of him? How would I prepare him to survive it? To resist it? Could he do both?

Erella's article on Women in Black in *Ha'aretz* helps me sort through the complexities of gender and power here. She talks about the importance of Women in Black's body language—women standing on the open streets, rather than in the expected organizational settings, such as political parties, women's organizations, or elective bodies; women wearing black rather than the white which usually symbolizes both female purity and peace. "The unconventional combination of being a woman, being in the public realm, and engaging in struggle undermines the conventional perception of what is a woman and what is a political struggle, and redefines them." (p. 2) It is the uncommon juxtapositions of symbolizations that marks Women in Black: women wearing black, standing in silence, mourning death—these are familiar images, readily understood within conventional feminine imagery. But to be located in such a public place, unprotected by the norms of interaction regulating conduct in more traditional spaces, holding signs that insist on a kind of speech that many see as taboo. . . these practices interrupt the familiar imagery:

> Women in Black struggle unintentionally with the significance of two central concepts in cultural experience: women and politics and the connection between them. In their protest, they undermine the conventional perception of these two concepts, launch a discourse about their significance, and suggest a new way of conceptualization. (p. 1)

The day after speaking with Erella, Gili and I met again with Tamar and Saret, spoke again with them of Women in Black. They continue to gnaw at the question of why all these militant women in Women in Black don't call themselves feminists. My hunch is that the ideological horizon in Israel is already crowded with potent candidates: Zionism, socialism, pacifism, fundamentalism, nationalism. Strong and active women come to Women in Black with already existing political identities produced out of the prevailing alternatives; in a sense, there is no room for feminism. Only among lesbians does there seem to be a strong feminist identity; perhaps because the lesbians, if they come out, are pushed out of the other identity brackets by the rampant homophobia here. Or perhaps because many of the lesbians have immigrated from the U.S., bringing lesbian feminism with them. These are speculations, which Tamar and Saret have also entertained; but they are looking to their interviews for answers. I want to hear what they find.

We returned to the kibbutz by bus, on a warm summer evening, watching the sun play across the golds, greens and tans of the countryside. The abandoned buildings, surrounded by carefully tended fields and industrious kibbutzim, still haunt me. I wonder if there are Arab families in camps in Gaza, still holding the keys to these lost homes. Coming back to the kibbutz is like coming home, especially for Gili, but for me too. I could live here, in this doubled place. I think often of Narkis, her straightforward love for her kibbutz. She is not confined here; she embraces her locale. She is at home, unambiguously, while I flounder between longing for and being wary of such a home.

*****

WHO SHALL HAVE the last word in this journal? Should it go to Gili's mother, who flatly denies any possibility of peace? "They've always hated us and we've always hated them," she says. Admitting that it is impossible to kill all the Arabs, she nonetheless sees no alternative to continued fighting. Her resignation is self-serving, and self-destructive; it holds in abeyance any need to rethink, to reorient, to struggle for change, while chaining her to the very conditions that make her fear for the lives of her grandsons. Should it go to Aria, whose resignation is somewhat more specific? He claims that now is not a good time for peace, that there is no one to make peace with, because the Palestinians are so fragmented, Hamas is on the rise, the PLO fractured from within. "They will continue to try to kill us," he maintains, "and we will continue to try and catch them." His language captures the legitimacy of law and order for his side (they only "catch criminals"), while relegating the others to the ranks of the murderers. Again, it is a self-serving and self-destructive resignation; it refuses to think of possibilities, only of limits. If genuine peace is approached, perhaps the attraction of Hamas and other religious extremist groups will decline.

Or shall the last word go to Gila, who sees in the strength of the Meretz vote, and of Labor generally, (even in the occupied territories nearly 20% of the Jewish settlers voted for Labor!) a strong longing for peace, and willingness to compromise, among a majority of Israelis. Gila works tirelessly for peace. Her optimism is contagious; unfortunately, so is the pessimism of the others.

I think I will give the last word to Narkis, who neither hates nor sympathizes with the other; she is indifferent, in a mildly negative way, unless moved to fear or care by a particular episode. "I don't like them and they don't like me," she says. "Let them have the territories; I don't want them." She goes about her business, caring for her home, her family, her work, her kibbutz, shrugging her shoulders at the things that are beyond her capacity to effect. Narkis has come to represent for me a possible point of entry into the dangerous terrain housing adversarial identities. Her way of living suggests a selective forgetting, a partial disengagement from historical investments and authoritative words. This distancing gesture might lead toward uncoupling identity from its territorial obsessions, making room to create stories less dependent upon antagonism toward otherness.

It is hard to imagine how the heritage of the Holocaust, or of three generations of Palestinians living in the dismal camps in Gaza, could make room for cultivation of her focus. Nor is it easy to see her perspective competing successfully with the hegemonic identity practices produced and circulated so vigorously by the Israeli state and society. Still, perhaps, in this region of passions and counterpassions, of blood and grief and history, in indifference to otherness, and refusal of inheritance, may lie the possibility of peace.

Epilogue

August 28, 1993

LAST NIGHT I dreamed about the Holocaust.

I was driving down a long straight road, in an orderly procession of cars and police. The road ended at a river. We waited there for boats to take us across. Oren and I stood with my friend Elizabeth and her son Lee. Where were Gili and Ari? Maybe they got away.

At first it seemed that we were escaping, but we were not.

I was reading a novel, and I was completely absorbed in the book. We waded through water to the top of a ridge. I said to a companion that if this is the worst thing that ever happens to me, that won't be so bad. The woman, who was childless, agreed.

At the top of the ridge police separated the children and the adults. No one older than eighteen could accompany the children. The police stripped the children naked and began to examine them roughly.

I remained absorbed in my book. When I looked up, the children were gone.

I cried to Elizabeth that I did not see Oren go—what did he look like? She said he was stiff and frightened. "I didn't say good-bye," I sobbed. She demanded, sternly, "I said good-bye to Lee. Do you think that makes me feel any better?"

Elizabeth, usually so gentle, joined with the other mothers in scolding me for reading while the children were being taken away. "I couldn't help it," I cried. "It was my escape."

"You shouldn't have demanded an escape," they accused.

"I didn't demand it. It was there and I took it."

The women were taken to a set of offices, where we were stripped and put through a bureaucratic routine. I saw my old boss sitting behind a desk. He had become a Nazi bureaucrat. He pretended not to know me. I whispered desperately to him in Yiddish, asking where they took the children. He did not reply.

I WOKE TO the early morning sound of Oren scavenging in the cupboard for breakfast. I went and sat with him in the living room while he munched fig bars. We discussed cheetahs (currently his favorite animal) while I wrote down my dream. The dream's disquieting imagery has stayed with me all day. I can't begin to unpack the possibilities of meaning that the dream offers (including the wonderful irony of my former (Jewish) boss in Nazi uniform), but its troubling echo calls me back to this journal. Whatever else is going on, at some level Israel's authoritative word is speaking to/through me. It is hard to know how to respond, impossible not to try.

We've been back in Hawaii for over a year. I have found it difficult here to locate myself in relation to Israel and to this journal. In some ways I feel more Israeli here than I ever did on the kibbutz. I suppose that is predictable, since the parts of me that are most firmly lodged in the relations and events of Israel are the parts most foregrounded by their dislocation. Identity seems to be primarily made up of contrasts and relationships, a jostling patchwork of presences and absences. The missing voices are the ones that speak the loudest. Yet in other ways, Israel is receding, crowded out by the detail and detritus of daily life in another place. Like my slowly eroding grasp of Hebrew, my groundedness in Israel slips away. Yet, just as Ari sometimes surprises me by peppering his toddler babble with Hebrew words and phrases, I often surprise myself with a surge of partisan feelings for the place I never ceased to criticize when I was there.

For awhile I became a news junkie for anything having to do with Israel, compiling vast disorganized files that lay untended as I rushed on to the next bit of information. Weekly phone calls to Gili's folks were no balm. Compressed and overcoded long distance conversations only highlight the dense missing fabric of a life left behind.

I could not find a writerly voice to bring completion to this journal so long as I was straining back toward our lives in Israel. Writing is a highly embodied act; it is located in the flesh. Writing from where you are not is like sustained ventriloquism, and I find that I cannot throw my voice that far. On the kibbutz I ate my meals with 400 other people, walked everywhere, seldom handled money, explored a foreign language, and struggled to negotiate an unfamiliar and evocative set of identity claims. Here I am reimmersed in the nuclear family, the money economy, and the paid labor force, not to mention a set of gender, racial and national identity claims that are no less complex or problematic but are less visible to me because they are so familiar. I cannot write as if I were still in Israel. The distance from the near-desert to the subtropics is a journey of both the body and the spirit.

September 14

RABIN AND ARAFAT shaking hands on the White House lawn! Yesterday they signed a peace accord providing for Palestinian self-rule in the Gaza Strip and the West Bank town of Jericho, and promised to negotiate the status of the entire occupied territories over the next five years.

It is a tremendous first step toward peace. Gaza is a dismal toilet of a place, its economy choked by Israeli restrictions and miserable refugee camps. But it used to boast a respectable international port and a thriving citrus industry. The right amounts of financial aid, properly placed, could bring Gaza's economy back to life. The inclusion of Jericho in the agreement brings the West Bank into the negotiations, even if only in a small way. At last, it is possible to hope for concrete steps toward peace.

September 20

MY HEART SANK as I read Edward Said's piece in *The Nation* today on the peace accord. While not completely dismissive, Said is full of doubts. He points out that Arafat's leadership is precarious, his consultation with other Palestinians virtually nonexistent. He questions continued Israeli control over the land, water, security, and external relations of the autonomous areas. He is not sanguine about future negotiations on the remaining occupied territories.

While I respect Said a great deal, I feel myself furiously resisting his pessimistic tone. Aren't a few small steps toward settlement better than none at all? Of course many questions remain, and it is the job of Palestinian intellectuals such as Said to raise them - but can't I still be permitted a measure of optimism? I feel toward the peace accord the way C. Wright Mills once indicated that he felt toward socialism in Cuba: I worry with it, not about it. The cycle of hope and despair in Israeli politics is exhausting, even at a distance. I can't give up my expectations just yet.

September 23

GILI'S PARENTS TELL us that there is a heightened degree of tension on the kibbutz these days, along with a growing sense of hope. The thefts of cattle and equipment continue, and are always attributed to "Arabs from Gaza." On a neighboring kibbutz someone raised a Palestinian flag, alarming everyone about the obvious breach of security. The growing sense of danger is a continuation of the problems preceding the accord. Dov sent us a copy of the regional paper, *Col ha Darom* (All the South) containing an extensive article about our kibbutz. Photos of familiar faces—Natan, Yoram, Sadeh, Ron—gaze at us as Gili helps me struggle through the Hebrew. Our friends lament the increasing insecurity, and complain that they receive no help from higher authorities. Their greatest fear is that the insurgents will go from stealing to killing. They ask what they have to do to get attention to their predicament; does someone have to die before we are heard? Natan's wife, Sarah, speaks her fears: "The terrorists can bump into my kids by mistake. When we wake up in the morning and the bicycle has disappeared, we know that someone was here last night. Everybody lives with this fear. But somehow we get used to it."

At the same time, Dov sounds optimistic—hopeful

that perhaps some resolution can be found. Batsheva continues to be skeptical of any chances for peace in her lifetime. The general climate of opinion on the kibbutz favors the accord.

October 7

THE WINNERS OF this year's Right Livelihood Award include Arna Mer-Khanis, the Israeli teacher who was arrested for her work in Palestinian schools. The Right Livelihood Award acknowledges grassroots work that improves people's lives in practical ways. She shares the award with Mary and Carrie Dann, sisters in the Western Shoshone tribe who are fighting to preserve their land and way of life; and Vandana Shiva, Indian feminist and environmental activist. I've used books and films by and about all these people in my feminist theory class; I feel like my class just got this award.

October 23

RECENTLY IN MY feminist theory reading group we discussed Mary Layoun's literary analysis of *The Cactus*, a novel by Sahar Khalifeh, a Palestinian woman writer. Layoun praises the female protagonist in the story for bringing a multi-voiced perspective to the Palestinian-Israeli conflict. This character, a Palestinian peasant woman named Umm Sabir, witnessed the assassination of an Israeli army officer by a Palestinian resistance fighter. While approving of the killing, she expressed sympathy for the bereaved wife and daughter. Umm Sabir's compassion toward the Israeli woman and child suggests to Layoun a potential retelling of the story of Palestinian identity. Umm Sabir traverses the boundaries between what is inside and what is outside; she complicates simple divisions between "them" and "us."

After our meeting I became increasingly disturbed, not by the article or the story, but by our discussion of it. We focused on the exciting intellectual approach the author employed, and the political promise that might lie in the ability to combine commitment to a struggle with compassion for the enemy. Only later did it occur to me that the Israeli army officer was voiceless throughout this narrative. He was an iconic representation of The Oppressor. While the grief of the woman and child were regrettable, the death of the man was not. But who could this man have been? Aviv? Omer? Baruch? Less personally, what politics could he represent? In a country with a citizen army, an army officer could literally be anyone. His wife was probably a former soldier, his daughter a future one. Perhaps the dead man was one of the many military officers active in Peace Now. Or a reluctant reservist forced into duty in the territories, protecting Jewish settlers whose political agenda he despised. Or perhaps not. But this dead officer was no one at all, just an empty representation of The Enemy, a faceless, voiceless soon-to-be-corpse. No multivocality for him.

November 3

NIZA JUST SENT me a copy of her paper on racism among Israeli Jewish girls. It is a fascinating account of the differences in the life worlds of secular and religious adolescent girls. Niza reports on several studies documenting increasing feelings of hatred toward Arabs among Jewish youth in Israel (40% of the young people questioned in a 1988 survey indicated that they felt hatred for most or all Arabs, compared to 32% in 1974). Within these general figures, religious girls expressed the greatest racial hatred (63%) while secular girls espoused the least (28%). (For males, the figures were 32% for secular boys and 50% for religious.)

Based on in-depth interviews with secular and religious girls, Niza finds that the secular girls, who also hate and fear Arabs and identify with Zionist goals, live in a world which admits of competing claims about morality and politics. They inhabit discourses that combine Jewish nationalism and the mandates of militarized identities with universal claims about human rights, national self-determination, and individual moral autonomy. The girls respond to these clashing imperatives by finding their own way through them, doing the intellectual and emotional work necessary to negotiate competing claims.

Religious girls, in contrast, live in a much more consistent world. They inhabit a discourse that provides clear-cut rules of thinking, feeling and acting. The boundaries between "us" and "them" are obvious. "They" are hateful and untrustworthy by nature, while "we" are rational, humane, and fully entitled to the place "we" desire in the world. Amplifying their clear and unified identity as Jews is an equally one dimensional identity as females, which is based in their religion's dictates concerning female modesty and chastity. Niza says that the religious girls experience "the street as a place of danger and the body as the locus of injury." (p. 20) The presence of Arabs in public space threatens their modesty and purity; the possibility of defilement looms large. Niza sees their expressions of hatred as part of a search for control, an effort to establish the social markers that can secure the girls' proper place in the ordered world of family, religion, and society.

As I read Niza's account of her conversations with religious girls, I am reminded of several recent televised interviews with Jewish settlers in the occupied territories. Niza contains her rage; I do not. "Who do they think they are?" I demand indignantly. But that's precisely the problem, isn't it? It is in the processes by which people create who they are that this unabashed sense of entitlement, and accompanying invisibility or demonization of peoples or histories inconvenient to those attachments, is produced. In "The Women Next Door," Israeli filmmaker Michal Aviad interviews Aliza, a Jewish woman who has made *aliyah* (immigrated) from the U.S. to the West Bank. Aliza describes the land upon which her family has built their home: "There was nothing here." No acknowledgment that her Palestinian neighbors grazed their animals on the hills she claims; no acceptance of any other way to relate to a land and its history. This woman steps outside of the frame of self-understanding Niza found in religious girls; she calls herself a feminist, and resents the Israeli feminist movement's opposition to the occupation. "Those are two separate issues," she insists. Her unconventional ideas regarding gender equality do not interrupt her hostility to "the Arabs," whom she regards as "primitive" and "uncivilized." Her feminism and her nationalism may, in a backhanded way, reinforce each other, coupling around a shared sense of daring and defiance: "We see ourselves on the front line."

Niza's research offers a cautionary tale to me as a parent: don't surround your children too completely with like-minded people and ideas, or they will not learn the crucial skills of negotiating complex and contradictory social spaces. To truly value diversity, children must encounter it. A certain amount of turbulence and contention can enrich children's ability to appreciate otherness and to make their own way. But Aliza, the serious young racist feminist, provokes a different parental anxiety: that appreciation of difference is a fragile and vulnerable thing, easily swallowed up by the stubborn and seductive demands of self-interest and self-justification. One might expect Aliza's self-understandings to contain some turbulence, to call themselves into question; her belief in equality between men and women surely does not go down well in the settler movement. But she seems to have pinned identity down neatly around the religious dictates of Israeli national destiny. Somehow she evades the complexities that Niza's secular girls faced, although her world seems to contain them. In the complex process of enabling one's children to navigate competing identity claims, there are unfortunately no guarantees.

November 18

I HAVE JUST read a very disturbing article on reproductive technology in Israel. In "Anything for a Baby: Reproductive Technology in Israel" Alison Solomon writes:

> Reproductive technology is widely employed in Israel. For its population of 4 million, Israel has 16 *In-Vitro* Fertilization (IVF)—"test tube baby"—clinics. Fourteen of them are public, giving Israel more publicly-funded clinics per capita than any other country in the world. For example, Australia, one of the leaders in reproductive technology, has 17 clinics for a population of 15 million. Treatment in Israeli public clinics is free, [for Israeli Arabs too? Solomon doesn't say] and there are no waiting lists. Israeli doctors are among the foremost in the field, and the technologies used are the most up to date available; Israel was

> the first country to enable a woman without fallopian tubes to become pregnant and give birth." (p. 102)

She goes on to locate this love affair with reproductive technology within a long-standing public obsession with fertility. When Israeli politicians talk about the "demographic problem," they usually refer to the Arab birthrate (higher than the Jewish one) and the specter of an Arab majority within the Jewish state. (Palestinians echo the dictates of the "demographic race" by urging women to have large families so as to "contribute to the struggle.") The Israeli government pursues numerous pro-natalist policies, including subsidizing large families, neglecting birth control technologies, and producing moral exhortations to women to procreate out of patriotism. These agendas for reproduction were explicitly linked to *in vitro* fertilization by a Knesset member, and former IDF Chief-of-Staff, "who stated that, although IVF was expensive, it was still cheaper than the cost of bringing in new immigrants." (p. 103)

Israel's massive commitments to Jewish births suggest a macabre match for its efficiency in creating the machinery of death. The "life" most at stake seems to be that of the state, not the people. In "The Woman Next Door" several tearful mothers (and one father) accompany their sons to the army induction center as the young men begin their obligatory three years of service. "I'm scared my son is going to change," cries one woman, lamenting the psychological costs of policing the Palestinians. The young men shuffling fearfully or brazenly into the induction center mirror in some odd way the women flocking to the IVF centers. More Jewish births equal more Israeli soldiers equal a more powerful state. Absent from this Spartan formula are the women whose bodies undergo the invasive technology, whose lives are spent raising the children (or enduring the pity reserved for women without children), who then are expected to deliver them to the state and send them off to war.

December 19

THIS IS ONE hell of a peace process. Withdrawal of Israeli troops from the occupied territories was supposed to begin on December 13. It did not. Not even a token withdrawal. Negotiations have stalled on differing definitions of the size of Jericho (the PLO claims 136 square miles, while Israel recognizes only 35 square miles), on who has police power in the autonomous areas, and on who controls the border crossings from Jordan to Jericho and from Egypt to Gaza. Forty six Palestinians and fourteen Israelis have died since September 13 in the violent struggles against the peace accord. Israeli undercover troops have killed several Palestinian activists, including the very popular guerrilla leader Imad Aqel, and Fatah Hawk Ahmed Abu Rish, who had surrendered his arms a few days earlier and been taken off the wanted list. Five high-ranking PLO representatives have been assassinated since September 13. Several Palestinian factions united by their opposition to the PLO have joined forces to undermine the accord.

The *Jerusalem Post* (international edition) offers a numbing litany of violence and counter violence. A young Israeli kindergarten teacher, Shalva Ozana, and a yeshiva student, Yitzhak Weinstock, were killed in a drive-by shooting near Hebron. Settlers from Kiryat Arba killed one Palestinian and injured five others in retribution. The paper reports that IDF soldiers stood by while Jewish settlers fired on Arabs, some of whom had thrown rocks at the Israelis. No arrests were made. The paper routinely describes the Arabs as terrorists, the Jews as settlers. Shulamit Aloni, head of Meretz, the party Gili and I supported in the 1992 election, accuses the government of "double-talk" in "vowing to crack down on the settlers but failing to order the security forces to act against them." (December 11, p. 4)

The November 13th *Jerusalem Post* (international edition) mentions a leaflet circulating among Israeli soldiers urging them to disobey possible future orders to evacuate settlements. The leaflet calls on troops not to "be a partner to the uprooting of Jewish settlements." (p. 5) I am reminded of the national trauma surrounding the evacuation of Yammit. Yammit was a Jewish settlement in the Sinai, evacuated in April, 1982 as part of the Israeli-Egyptian peace treaty. The town of 8,000 was dismantled by Israeli troops, and those settlers and their supporters who refused to leave were forcibly removed. In his poignant book *In the Land of Israel* Amos Oz talks with a veteran of Yammit, Pinchas Wallerstein, who became a prominent leader in Gush Emunim. Wallerstein remembers Yammit with bitterness as the first time the Israeli government "broke the Zionist taboo against uprooting a Jewish settlement." (p. 113)

A curious counter memory: Sidra DeKoven Ezrahi writes in "Between the Lines: To Beit Sahur and Back" of a dialogue between Jewish residents of Jerusalem and Palestinians in Beit Sahur: "On one of our visits to Beit Sahur, the young son of our Palestinian host looked around the crowded room impatiently and asked his father what had happened to the Jews who were supposed to arrive. His father pointed to the people sitting on the couch. 'No,' the boy insisted. 'They're not Jewish; they don't have guns.'"(p. 35)

In these asymmetrical memories of bitterness and vulnerability I hear a prelude to the coming crisis. There is a powerful taboo on Jews policing Jews, on Jewish tanks bulldozing Jewish homes on land some Jews claim as theirs. Combined with this reluctance is an institutionalized indifference to Jews policing Palestinians; it is commonplace for those same tanks to raze Arab homes. Rabin's peace initiative will require recalibration of both these practices; Israeli troops will be restricted in their power over (some) Palestinians, and compelled to exercise power over (some) other Jews. It will not be an easy shift.

January 11, 1994

THE NEWS REPORTS on the peace process are often intensely irritating. The ubiquitous first person plural of Israeli society, that aggressive "we" haunted by a thousand particulars, is caricatured and disguised by the assertions about "Israel" I read and hear daily. The monoglossic language of state identity dominates the stage: "Israel" did this, "Israel" said that, "Israel" stood up to something or backed down from something else. Where, in this fiction of a monolithic state actor, are the many intricate voices of that entangled and dissonant place? Where are the complexities and ambiguities of the Israelis I know?

Accounts of Israel in the U.S. news, which I still gobble up with a greedy yet disdainful eagerness, persist in two kinds of ignorant interpretations. The first usually comes from left-of-center sources, and collapses the complexities of Israeli politics toward the left. On numerous occasions I have heard or read criticism of the peace accord on the grounds that "the Palestinians got too little, and the Israelis got everything they wanted." While the Palestinians did, as yet, get too little, who are these Israelis who "got everything they wanted"? What about the many thousands who feel that any territorial compromise is a violation of a sacred trust, or a suicidal retreat from an implacable foe? What about the 100,000 plus settlers in the West Bank and Gaza, many of them armed and determined not to leave? Most of the settlers do not think of themselves as living in contested territory, but as reclaiming ancient Judea and Samaria for the Jewish people. The international edition of the *Jerusalem Post* reports on a current operation called "This is My Land," in which Jewish settlers are establishing 130 new "presences" on the West Bank to undermine the possibilities of withdrawal. They are certainly not preparing to leave, nor did they "get everything they wanted." Beyond the settlers themselves, what about the half of the country that routinely votes for Likud or the parties farther right? What about the drivers who yell "whores of Arafat" at Women in Black? These Israelis did not "get everything they wanted." "Land for peace" is a swap that the Rabin government is risking, but for many Israelis "greater Israel" is not up for trade.

The second pervasive simplification, coming both from leftist and from more establishment sources, routinely represents Israel as if it were an extension of the U.S. on the Mediterranean. Those among the Israelis and Palestinians who are opposed to the peace accord are characterized as isolated extremists, the lunatic fringe. "Extremists seek to block accord through violence," proclaimed a recent headline in the local paper. All the reasonable people in the Middle East want peace, so the story goes, while a few radicals on both sides are obstacles to the accord. While I agree that it is reasonable for both Jews and Arabs to want peace, this image of a large homogeneous political center contrasted to a detached and marginal extreme severely misrepresents the extensive divisions tearing through Israel, and disuniting Palestinians as well. What sense does it make to characterize the settlers as "the lunatic fringe of Israeli politics," as did a recent editorial in *The Nation,* when the Likud government for the last decade (and Labor before them) sponsored those settlers, diverting huge amounts of the national budget to creating and sustaining the settlements while protecting them from both internal criticism and Arab sabotage? Shamir admitted after his 1992 defeat by Labor that his plan all along had been to populate the occupied territories with so many Jews that the regions would be reincorporated into Israel by default, overwhelmed by the weight of Jewish villages and American money. Thousands of people moved to the territories to buy cheap homes and commute to work along brand new roads, while within Israel housing is increasingly unaffordable and the transportation infrastructure crumbles from neglect. One might take comfort in calling the settlers "lunatic," but they are hardly "fringe."

February 18

THE MOST RECENT *Nation* has a fascinating article by Edward Said. He calls on Palestinians to thank Arafat and company for their work and then create new political structures and new leaders through collective deliberation. While Said continues to be pessimistic about the possibilities of peace, his anger and anguish is here directed mostly toward fellow Palestinians—against current PLO leadership for corruption and lack of a mass political base, against Diaspora Palestinians for their minimal support of the national cause, against individual Palestinians who substitute isolated personal actions for collective response.

What most intrigued me about Said's essay is the forthright interdependence of Jewish and Palestinian histories and politics. He looks to Jewish successes to model Palestinian policy. The early Zionist settlers focused on concrete and measurable gains: "Another dunum, another goat." Contemporary Israeli negotiators are armed with specific maps, plans, and resources. Said wants the Palestinians to follow this example, to substitute "the discipline of detail" for grandiose sentiments lacking in particulars.(p. 191)

When people are urged to follow the example of their enemy, shouldn't that advice erode any easy or complete distinctions between the two? How do the categories "Palestinian" and "Jew" stay so far apart, how do people sustain their sense of moral superiority and entitlement, when one is evoked, even in this limited way, as a model for the other?

April 8

WHATEVER REMAINED OF the peace process seems to be shredding in the cold wind of rancid bitterness and revenge. On February 25 a settler from Kiryat Arba entered the Tomb of the Patriarchs, the 2000 year old shrine in Hebron where the prophet Abraham is said to be buried, and killed several dozen Muslim worshippers, wounding scores more (exact numbers are uncertain). It is not clear what the security people were doing, but they certainly didn't get in the way of Baruch Goldstein, who fired methodically on the crowd with an automatic rifle until he was beaten to death by the survivors. Goldstein left a suicide note proclaiming his love of Israel.

A month later, on the annual commemoration of Holocaust Day, eight Israelis were killed and many more wounded when a bomb exploded at a bus stop. The dead included three teen age girls. The next day a drive-by shooting in Ashdod killed one, wounded four. Ashdod is near our kibbutz. These are only the most visible assaults—there have been dozens of clashes, uncertain numbers killed and wounded, during the last few weeks. Hamas has promised to turn Israel into a war zone during the week of the Independence Day ceremonies.

It already is a war zone, framed by the bitter recriminations that turn grief into hate. Baruch Goldstein didn't start all this either, of course; he was driven to revenge, say his friends, by his grief at the death of loved ones at Palestinian hands. And of course those Palestinians didn't start it either, since in Palestinian eyes all the settlers are aggressors. Voices on both sides call for pulling out of the peace process to "punish the other side"—what about the punishment they deal to themselves? Does no one flinch at how much they resemble their enemies?

My hunger for news of Israel is being eroded by dread. I know that there must still be voices of dissent and criticism coming from within Israel, but I cannot hear them. If we were still in Israel I imagine that I could join what must be an agitated national debate about the peace process: the steadfast presence of Women in Black, or Narkis's calm local allegiances, could offer counterpoint to the litany of violence. But the heteroglossic din of that diverse land does not travel across the wire services. Only the staccato drill of murder and counter-murder reach us here. Oren was puzzled and alarmed when I pulled the car over and burst into tears as the news of the Holocaust Day murders came over the radio. I tried to explain about the war, about the destructiveness of revenge, about the courage it takes to make peace. The words sounded hollow to me; I wonder how they sound to him.

April 15

GILI SAYS THAT the word "stubborn" in Hebrew refers to

someone who sticks with his position after he changes his mind. I used to think that was funny.

The *Jerusalem Post* is full of analyses of the massacre in the mosque at the tomb of Abraham. The March 19 front-page headline screams "Hebron massacre 'might have been prevented if not for security lapse.'" Acting OC Central Command Major-General Danny Yatom testified to the Shamgar Commission that terrorism has always been something Arabs do to Jews, not vice versa. "I look at the overall picture of Arab attacks against Jews and Jewish attacks against Arabs—and on the one side there are hundreds, while on the other, a few isolated incidents.... A crazy act like this isn't something we expected in light of our accumulated experience." (p. 1) Yatom further told the commission that the army had never discussed the possibility of Jewish terrorism.

At first I am incredulous: where has this guy been? Who could possibly believe such a thing? But on reflection, I suspect his response is not disingenuous. The militarized definitions of identity prevalent in Israel reserve political legitimacy exclusively for Jews; actions of the Israeli state are never seen as terrorist, no matter who is hurt or how. Their violence may be regrettable, but it is accepted by most Israeli Jews as necessary. Israelis act to preserve a legitimate social order. Palestinians, on the other hand, have no such claim to any legitimate social order, so their violence is by definition illegitimate; no appeals to necessity are acceptable for them.

Baruch Goldstein's murder of the worshippers at the mosque seems to the Israeli authorities to be completely unlike the actions of the IDF and border police in the territories. Goldstein was outside the law; his actions provoked the state to declare the Kach and Kahane Hai movements (with which he was affiliated) to be illegal terrorist organizations. Of course it is encouraging that most Israelis condemned Goldstein's actions, and that the state has taken some action against its far-right wing. But in the process the airtight distinction between state violence and illegitimate terrorism has been reinforced. Goldstein's murders were outside the law, illegal; the occupation is not. Never mind that Goldstein was wearing a military uniform; never mind that a country with a citizen army has irretrievably blurred the boundary between military and civilian practices. Never mind that, to Palestinian eyes, fine distinctions between legal and illegal Jewish violence are irrelevant and self-serving.

One grim comic note inserted itself into the headlines: the specter of Jesse Jackson trying to inspire young Palestinian men with the message of the U.S. civil rights movement, and instead finding himself caught in an exchange of rocks, tear gas and rubber bullets. Jackson tried to get the crowd to exchange the chant "God is Great" for "Keep hope alive." Somewhere in the background must have been "Give peace a chance." Fat chance.

April 18

GILI'S FATHER REPORTS that the local organization of kibbutzim has at last gotten attention to its security problems from central military and political authorities. The state is building a new security fence along the border between Israel and Gaza. The people on our kibbutz are relieved that some action is being taken. Another barbed wire fence is erected. Another set of guards is posted. Another border is fortified.

Selected Bibliography

The Academic Study Group on Israel and the Middle East, 25 Lyndale Avenue, London, NW2 2QB (November, 1991).

Alcalay, Ammiel, *After Jews and Arabs: Remaking Levantine Culture* (Minneapolis: University of Minnesota Press, 1993).

Bakhtin, M. M., *The Dialogic Imagination* (Michael Holquist, ed.; Caryl Emerson and Michael Holquist, trans.) (Austin: University of Texas Press, 1981).

Bhabha, Homi K., "DissemiNation: time, narrative, and the margins of the modern nation," in Homi Bhabha, ed., *Nation and Narration* (Routledge, 1990), pp. 291-322.

Binur, Yoram, *My Enemy, My Self* (New York: Penguin 1989).

Boyarin, Jonathan, *Storm from Paradise: The Politics of Jewish Memory* (Minneapolis: University of Minnesota Press, 1992).

Butler, Judith, "Imitation and Gender Insubordination," in Diana Fuss, ed., *Inside/Out: Lesbian Theories and Gay Theories* (New York: Routledge, 1991), pp. 13-31.

Elon, Amos, "The Politics of Memory," *New York Review of Books* (vol XI, no 16), Oct 7, 1993: 3-5.

Espanioly, Nabila, "Palestinian Women in Israel Respond to the *Intifada*," in Barbara Swirski and Marilyn Safir, eds., *Calling the Equality Bluff* (New York: Pergamon Press, 1991), pp. 147-151.

Ezrahi, Sidra DeKoven, "Between the Lines: To Beit Sahur and Back," in Rita Falbel, Irena Klepfisz, and Donna Nevel, eds., *Jewish Women's Call for Peace* (New York: Firebrand Books, 1990), pp. 35-38.

Falbel, Rita, Irena Klepfisz, & Donna Nevel, eds., *Jewish Women's Call for Peace: A Handbook for Jewish Women on the Israeli/Palestinian Conflict* (Ithaca, New York: Firebrand Books, 1990).

Friedman, Marcia, *Exile In the Promised Land* (Ithaca, New York: Firebrand Books, 1990).

Gibson, James William, *The Perfect War* (Boston, New York: Atlantic Monthly Press, 1986).

Gilad, Lisa, *Ginger and Salt: Yemeni Jewish Women in an Israeli Town* (Boulder, Colorado: Westview Press, 1989).

Goldberg, David Theo, and Michael Krausz, eds., *Jewish Identity* (Philadelphia: Temple University Press, 1993).

Golan, Galia, conversation, June 8, 1992.

Gould, Janet, "The Problem of Being 'Indian': One Mixed-Blood's Dilemma," in Sidonie Smith and Julia Watson, eds., *DeColonizing the Subject: The Politics of Gender in Women's Autobiography* (Minneapolis: University of Minnesota Press, 1992), pp. 81-87.

Grossman, David, *The Yellow Wind* (trans by Haim Watzman) (New York: Dell Publishing, 1978).

Haj, Samira, "Palestinian Women and Patriarchal Relations," *Signs* (17) Summer, 1992: 761-778.

Helman, Sarit, conversations, June 8 and July 19, 1992.

Hoenig, B., "Toward an Agonistic Feminism: Hannah Arendt and the Politics of Identity," in Judith Butler & Joan W. Scott, eds., *Feminists Theorize the Political* (New York: Routledge, 1992), pp. 215-235

Hubbell, Stephen, "Waiting in Gaza," *The Nation* (vol. 258, no. 1), January 3/10, 1994: 4-5.

Joeres, Ruth-Ellen Boetcher, "On Writing Feminist Academic Prose," *Signs* (Summer, 1992): 701-704.

Kimmerling, Baruch, and Sarit Helman, "Paradigmatic War Rationality and the Constitution of the 'Different' Rationality of the Lebanon War," Department of Sociology and Anthropology, Hebrew University of Jerusalem, unpublished paper.

Kundera, Milan, *The Unbearable Lightness of Being* (New York: Harper and Row, 1984).

Layoun, Mary, "Telling Spaces: Palestinian Women and the Engendering of National Narratives," in Andrew Parker, Mary Russo, Doris Summer and Patricia Yeager, eds., *Nationalisms and Sexualities* (New York: Routledge, 1992), pp. 407-423

Lipman, Beata, *Israel: The Embattled Land* (London: Pandora Press, 1988).

Lustick, Ian S., and Barry Rubin, eds., *Critical Essays on Israeli Society, Politics, and Culture* (Albany, New York: State University of New York Press, 1991).

Margalit, Avishai, "The Kitsch of Israel," *The New York Review of Books*, (November 24, 1988): 20-24.

Mar'i, Mariam, and Edna Zaretsky, "Women-in-Dialogue Tour," in Rita Falbel, Irena Klepfisz, and Donna Nevel, eds., *Jewish Women's Call for Peace* (New York: Firebrand Books, 1990), pp. 15-19.

Myers, Martha, "Inside the Intifada," *The Women's Review of Books* (vol. IX, no. 7), April, 1992: 15-16.

News From Within, special double issue: "Women under Jewish and Islamic Fundamentalism," (October-November, 1992) Alternative Information Center, P.O. Box 31417, Jerusalem.

Oz, Amos, *In the Land of Israel* (New York: Vintage Books, 1984).

Rapoport, Tamar, conversations June 8 and July 19, 1992.

Rapoport, Tamar, and Sarit Helman, "The Protest Vigil of Women in Black as Political Performance," School of Education and Department of Sociology and Anthropology, Hebrew University of Jerusalem, unpublished paper.

Said, Edward, "Arafat's Deal," *The Nation* (vol 257, no 8), September 10, 1993: 269-270.

Said, Edward, "Rally and Resist: For Palestinian Independence," *The Nation* (vol 258, no. 6), February 14, 1994: 190-193.

Schleifer, Yigal, "The Few, The Proud" *The Jerusalem Post Magazine* (July 19, 1992): 16-17.

The Seventh Day: Soldiers Talk about the Six-Day War (recorded and edited by a group of young Kibbutz members) (London: Andre Deutsch Limited, 1970).

Shadmi, Erella, "Politics Through the Back Door," *Ha'aretz* (February 24, 1992).

Shadmi, Erella, conversation, July 20, 1992.

Sharoni, Simona, "Rethinking Peace and Security from Women's Struggles: Feminist Perspectives on Peace Building in the Middle East," presented at the Fourteenth General Conference of the International Peace Research Association, Kyoto, Japan, July, 1992.

Sharoni, Simona, "To Be a Man in the Jewish State," *Challenge* (vol. 2, no. 5), September-October, 1991: 26-28.

Smith, Sidonie, and Julia Watson, eds., *DeColonizing the Subject: The Politics of Gender in Women's Autobiography* (Minneapolis: University of Minnesota Press, 1992).

Smith, Sidonie, "Who's Talking/Who's Talking Back: The Subject of Personal Narrative," *Signs* (vol. 18, no. 2), Winter, 1993: 392-407.

Solomon, Alison, "Anything for a Baby: Reproductive Technology in Israel," in Barbara Swirski and Marilyn Safir, eds., *Calling the Equality Bluff* (New York: Pergamon Press, 1991), pp. 102-107.

Spiegelman, Art, *Maus: A Survivor's Tale. I: My Father Bleeds History* (New York: Pantheon, 1973).

Spiegelman, Art, *Maus: A Survivor's Tale. II: And Here My Troubles Began* (New York: Pantheon, 1986).

Stiver, Camilla, "Reflections on the Role of Personal Narrative in Social Science," *Signs* (vol. 18, no. 2), Winter, 1993: 408-425.

Strum, Philippa, *The Women are Marching: The Second Sex and the Palestinian Revolution* (New York: Lawrence Hill Books, 1992).

Svirsky, Gila, conversation, May 1, 1992.

Svirsky, Gila, "Women in Black," in Rita Falbel, Irena Klepfisz, and Donna Nevel, eds., *Jewish Women's Call for Peace* (Ithaca, New York: Firebrand Books, 1990), pp. 8-9.

Swirski, Barbara and Marilyn P. Safir, eds., *Calling the Equality Bluff: Women in Israel* (New York: Pergamon Press, 1991).

Timmerman, Jacobo, *The Longest War: Israel in Lebanon* (Miguel Acoca, trans.) (New York: Vintage Books, 1982).

Todorov, Tzvetan, *Mikhail Bakhtin: The Dialogical Principle* (Wlad Godzich, trans.) (Minneapolis: University of Minnesota Press, 1984).

Trinh Minh-ha, *When the Moon Waxes Red* (New York: Routledge, 1991).

Trinh Minh-ha, *Woman, Native, Other* (Bloomington, Indiana: Indiana University Press, 1989).

Vitullo, Anita, "Yitzhak Rabin and Israel's Death Squads," *Middle East Report* (vol. 22, no. 5), September-October, 1992: 40-42.

Warnock, Kitty, *Land Before Honour: Palestinian Women in the Occupied Territories* (New York: Monthly Review Press, 1990).

Wolf, Aaron, *A Purity of Arms* (New York: Doubleday, 1989).

Women in Black National Newsletter (Women in Black, POB 6363, Jerusalem, Israel 91060).

Yanay, Niza, "National Hatred, Female Subjectivity, and the Boundaries of Cultural Discourse," Department of Behavioral Sciences, Ben Gurion University, Beer Sheva, Israel, unpublished paper.

Young, Elise, *Keepers of the History: Women and the Israeli-Palestinian Conflict* (New York: Teachers College Press, 1992).